Fostering Self-Efficacy in Higher Education Students

Palgrave Teaching and Learning

Series Editor: **Sally Brown**

Facilitating Work-Based Learning
Facilitating Workshops
For the Love of Learning
Fostering Self-Efficacy in Higher Education Students
Leading Dynamic Seminars
Learning, Teaching and Assessment in Higher Education
Live Online Learning
Masters Level Teaching, Learning and Assessment

Further titles are in preparation

Universities into the 21st Century

Series Editors: **Noel Entwistle and Roger King**

Becoming an Academic
Cultures and Change in Higher Education
Global Inequalities and Higher Education
Learning Development in Higher Education
Managing your Academic Career
Managing your Career in Higher Education Administration
Research and Teaching
Teaching Academic Writing in UK Higher Education
Teaching for Understanding at University
Understanding the International Student Experience
The University in the Global Age
Writing in the Disciplines

Palgrave Research Skills

Authoring a PhD
The Foundations of Research (2nd edn)
Getting to Grips with Doctoral Research
Getting Published
The Good Supervisor (2nd edn)
Maximizing the Impacts of University Research
The PhD Viva
The Postgraduate Research Handbook (2nd edn)
The Professional Doctorate
Structuring Your Research Thesis

You may also be interested in:

Teaching Study Skills and Supporting Learning

For a complete listing of all our titles in this area please visit
www.palgrave.com/studyskills

Fostering Self-Efficacy in Higher Education Students

Laura Ritchie

 macmillan education   palgrave

First published 2016 by
PALGRAVE

Palgrave in the UK is an imprint of Macmillan Publishers Limited, registered in England, company number 785998, of 4 Crinan Street, London, N1 9XW.

Palgrave Macmillan in the US is a division of St Martin's Press LLC, 175 Fifth Avenue, New York, NY 10010.

Palgrave is a global imprint of the above companies and is represented throughout the world.

Palgrave® and Macmillan® are registered trademarks in the United States, the United Kingdom, Europe and other countries.

ISBN 978–1–137–46377–7

This book is printed on paper suitable for recycling and made from fully managed and sustained forest sources. Logging, pulping and manufacturing processes are expected to conform to the environmental regulations of the country of origin.

A catalogue record for this book is available from the British Library.

A catalog record for this book is available from the Library of Congress.

Printed in China

To Ben, thank you for believing in me always.

Contents

Preface

Self-efficacy beliefs are at the core of every action that we all, whether teacher or student, undertake. These specific beliefs about perceptions of capability as related to individual tasks are not one of the most commonly talked about qualities of the self, but self-efficacy beliefs are fundamental to everything. As teachers in higher education, we strive to put students at the centre of learning and teaching, and understanding the formation and role of self-beliefs can have a huge impact on this process. Developing self-efficacy happens through communication and active learning, which facilitates a two-way interaction between learners and teachers. This fosters trust, so teachers and learners can risk having moments of vulnerability where we are willing to expand learning horizons and grow. Sometimes, perhaps, there will not instantly be success, but with guidance and reflection, these moments allow exploration, and as learners progress they can develop security in their beliefs through positive experiences. With established self-efficacy beliefs, students will have both the foundation and tools to successfully continue their learning after leaving the higher education environment.

As I became a more experienced teacher and researcher within higher education, I noticed there was not necessarily an equal focus on student self-efficacy beliefs across subjects. In some areas, students and teachers actively pursued building self-beliefs and discuss this openly, whereas in other areas self-efficacy was important but not spoken about, and in yet other disciplines it was not clear whether these beliefs were recognised as an essential part of the learning experience or not. Self-efficacy research continues to increase and find links with learning and performance that demonstrate its importance across disciplines.

This book explains and contextualises self-efficacy theoretically and within various teaching contexts, bringing a practical understanding of how these beliefs contribute to students' outlook, learning experiences, and achievement. Different types of learning in higher education are presented in Chapter 1, and a precedent is set for why it is important for teachers and students to be aware of self-efficacy and to cultivate these beliefs. Chapter 2 explains self-efficacy theory, and subsequent chapters address different practical ways that students and teachers can develop aspects of self-efficacy: through communication in Chapter 3, self-regulation and an awareness of learning process in Chapter 4, and the influence of class learning experiences in Chapter 5. The outward face of achievement, as it looks toward employment, is presented in Chapter 6. Finally, Chapter 7 challenges all of us to continue to develop our self-efficacy through learning, teaching, and professional life. Vignettes and case studies are drawn from across disciplines and presented throughout the book to demonstrate various practical applications of the principles and theory.

To avoid confusion with the many cultural gradations and designations of junior/senior teacher/lecturer, all who teach students in the context of higher education are in this book referred to as teachers. Similarly, the term class or classroom is used to avoid the exclusivity that can happen by designating a specific lecture, seminar, or class space.

There is no one, single answer that provides a definitive guide for how to foster these beliefs in all situations. Teachers are challenged to be active, demonstrating learning by being learners themselves, and working to allow themselves to be seen by their students as positive examples not only as teachers but also as learners. This volume provides an understanding of the nature of self-efficacy and the ways it can be influenced, developed, and reinforced, and it gives teachers the tools to actively facilitate student self-belief through learning and teaching.

Series Editor's Preface

▶ Palgrave Teaching and Learning

The Palgrave Teaching and Learning series for all who care about teaching and learning in higher education is designed with the express aim of providing useful, relevant, current, and helpful guidance on key issues in learning and teaching in the tertiary/post compulsory education sector. This is an area of rapid change, with higher education institutions reviewing and often implementing significant alterations in the ways they design, deliver, and assess the curriculum, taking into account not just innovations in how content is being delivered and supported, particularly through technological means, but also the changing relationships between academics and their students. The role of the teacher in higher education needs to be reconsidered when students can freely access content worldwide and seek accreditation and recognition of learning by local, national, or international providers (and may indeed prefer to do so). Internationally, students are becoming progressively more liable for the payment of fees, as higher education becomes seen as less of a public good and more of a private one, and this too changes the nature of the transaction. In many nations, the proportion of the population undertaking higher education is increasing, with consequent rethinking required on levels of independence and autonomy we can expect from sometimes formerly disadvantaged students.

Texts in this series address these and other emergent imperatives, with a deliberately international focus. The particular issues addressed in this book around fostering self-efficacy are ones that have particular currency at a time when we are encouraging students to engage ever more proactively in the learning process, so I am delighted to see this book in the series. Laura Ritchie is a UK National Teaching Fellow, so demonstrably an innovative, scholarly, and creative academic who inspires and enthuses others through her own creative spirit. I am delighted to include this volume in the Palgrave Teaching and Learning series.

Sally Brown
March 2015

Acknowledgements

Throughout the formulation and writing of this book there have been people, like Dr David Preston and Jonathan Worth, who have knowingly supported this project with interviews and indulged me in long discussions, and there have also been people who have encouraged me indirectly, like Dr and Dr Green, with the unexpected kindness of lending me their flat when I was abroad. I am deeply grateful to all who have crossed my path and been supportive. Specific thanks goes to Hans Jensen, for allowing me to observe his teaching, having lengthy discussions, and for believing in me before I even began this project, and to Kathleen Lasecki for supporting me both as a critic in reading many drafts of the text and as my mother. The support and enduring patience of my husband and children can never be quantified or adequately acknowledged. They sustain me.

1 The teaching environment in higher education

This chapter maps the landscape of learning within higher education, and the impact of the physical environment on learning and teaching is considered. There is a discussion of the understanding of excellence in education and the practicalities of achieving this by utilising resources to create situations where students and staff can flourish. A shift in perspective is encouraged with the introduction of the idea that academic work, including teaching and assessment, is like a performance that requires preparation and rehearsal. The teacher is called to be an active participant in teaching and learning processes through engagement, facilitation, and learning.

Learning happens everywhere. As thinking, breathing people experience their everyday lives they are exposed to countless situations where learning can happen. In higher education, teachers are privileged to be in a position where students come to learn. They *choose* to come. Education is required for youths, but applying to continue learning in higher education is a wilful choice made by students, and for teachers this presents a unique opportunity to shape and guide students' personal and intellectual development.

Learning can happen within lectures, in tutorials, among peers, in the dining hall, on the bus home, or in the space of someone's mind. Thinking about teaching in higher education conjures many different images, drawn from first-hand experiences, research, and of course, the media. A caricature might include a large lecture hall with someone wisely professing from a lectern or perhaps in front of a screen, and rows and rows of students listening intently or hunched over and frantically scribbling notes. Gerstein (2014) describes this old way of learning as being based on three Rs: receiving, responding, and regurgitating, where all students listen, copy notes down, and repeat information back. Fortunately much of that scenario is now archaic, but elements of the archetypal lecture with the direct transfer of knowledge still exits (Feden, 2012), and lecturing is one of the most prevalent forms of teaching in higher education (Smith & Valentine, 2012; Weimer, 2013). Teachers face challenges every day, whether with the group size, the room, the learning interface, or even their own unrecognised habit. In the world of that caricature, the lecturer held the knowledge and the students came, often to study with that particular person, to glean something about their subject. Because teachers are often bound by a given curriculum, and whether it is purposely designed by them or fixed by someone else to comply with requirements for that subject area, this can result in a limited approach to developing teaching practices.

Orienting ourselves towards excellence means constantly and actively improving the learning and teaching experience. Transparency of communication, inspiration for all learners, sustained motivation, transferrable meaning, and achievement are all qualities that are desired and found where education is at its best. Belief, motivation, creativity, and the skills to self-teach and effectively self-regulate learning can be evidenced in excellent teaching across various settings and disciplines. The underlying skills of decoding, analysing, organising, planning, and executing are universal. As we enhance our interface and work to understand the impact of learning on both attainment and, equally importantly, on each person as they develop, we step nearer to achieving this in our own teaching. When we allow ourselves to be open to new methodologies, and look beyond the context of the daily setting, to consider the underlying learning processes between the teacher and the student, we can unlock the best practice from across disciplines to enhance our own delivery.

▶ Critical distinctions: The push and pull of learning

A teacher can tell a student something, and there may or may not be understanding. If a series of instructions are given and it is clear that students are meant to follow those directions to completion, as a required task, then it is likely that they will do just that. This is especially likely as the students in question have specifically chosen their course, and have likely invested quite a lot of money in their tuition fees. The pattern of instructional teaching, imparting information and testing students on it, can create a culture where people learn to the test, and they also learn for the test. After a test, the students will feel accomplished, and wait for the next test. It can be like a dog that does tricks; it behaves well, but it needs to be led by the trainer. What happens when the trainer is gone? When the student leaves the institution? That halo effect from the leader will dissipate, and what is the student left with?

Communication, comprehension, and real student understanding are essential in teaching, so that when the opportunity arises for students to apply their knowledge and skill, they will be capable and equipped with all the tools they need. It is engrained in teachers to stretch and even push their students, but solely knowledge-based regurgitation is not representative of deep learning (Weimer, 2013). A more meaningful learning happens through focusing on the individual student experience, through doing, through mastery. When students achieve mastery, it must be something that they have done in their own right, with a sense of ownership and belief. This is seldom achieved through strictly lecture-based telling, with students taking notes with the sole aim of repeating the information back (Cousin, 2006). Deeper learning calls for something to come from the student, an impulse or creativity of thought that contributes and forms the learning. This is not suggesting creativity as in colourful multimedia displays, but in active, engaged thought that enables the student to go through the process of learning as a personal experience in which they feel a true sense of agency. When the teacher can present a structure or material in a way that allows space for this, then the student can be drawn into filling the void of their knowledge with experience.

For example, Stanford Professor Timothy Bresnahan (2012) explained how he allowed for this space in his teaching, literally creating a gap where he paused and stopped speaking. This vacuum within a lecture pulled students into the discussion and produced a situation where the students *needed* to respond. Specifically, he advised that the teacher should be passive at some points, and give control of the "floor" to the students. He advocated integrating silence after posing a problem or a question, and leaving a gap until the students reply, even if that gap feels awkward or lasts for several minutes. This requires assurance on the part of the teacher, as there is no guarantee how students might respond or if the discussion will follow the teacher's intended direction. Bresnahan emphasised that to create an active setting for the students, even in big lectures, the teacher must: 'know them, challenge them, liberate them' (Bresnahan, 2012). The teacher allows for student creativity, inquisitiveness, and for their experimentation, because they will not always know the desired or intended reply.

In traditional education, as students progress through the school system, there is a concept of authority that goes with teachers and their orientation as the figurehead of the classroom, which inevitably creates a student–teacher divide. Throughout primary and secondary education, students gain insight and experience and begin to close that gap that separates them from the teachers. For some students this happens seamlessly and naturally, but for others they may need to be guided by the teacher. Progressively, step by step, students can learn to recognise the process of their development and begin to understand, integrating reflection, and actively manage their personal transition as they claim deeper learning for their own.

Cousin (2006) proposes that this deeper learning occurs when students engage with 'threshold concepts'. These are concepts that are central to the discipline, and pivotal to making further connections across areas or the inner workings within a subject. Understanding a threshold concept allows students to unlock key aspects of understanding and begin to break barriers and build bridges that lead to mastery. These are difficult concepts for students, as they must do more than parrot back information, they must understand something that, on the surface, seems unlikely or causes them to shift their own perspective. Threshold concepts cannot be readily observed by simply paying attention to the surface of a situation. Once this understanding happens, the students can then make connections, and they gain a deeper understanding of the subject matter.

For example, in mathematics students must understand a threshold concept to make the jump from geometry, where area can be drawn and counted with a direct relationship to the numbers on the page, to understanding differential equations and integration. If the square in geometry has a side length of 3, it translates directly and the student can count 3 and produce the shape, but the conceptual understanding that occurs in calculus with differentiation and integration is not so straightforward and includes abstraction. A visual representation for equations can still be drawn, but it does not have a single-step connection to the numbers on the page. When the student understands the principle of what the equations mean, this threshold understanding is likely to be retained and remembered, allowing the student to be receptive to further learning and to integrate the concepts across other areas of their subject knowledge (Meyer, Land, & Davies, 2006). Wittgenstein, Anscombe, & Wright (1969) described the moment of understanding and described its related impacts when they said:

> When we first begin to believe something, what we believe is not a simple proposition, it is a whole system of propositions. (Light dawns gradually over the whole.) (p.21)

For students to be in a position to engage with these key concepts in their learning there needs to be space; space for them to respond to an impetus, to question, and to explore. The teacher must be aware that this threshold, the 'ah-ha', is a moment of personal understanding, and if the material and learning is catered to individual students, then although teachers cannot promise understanding, they can facilitate it. When students achieve mastery, and they understand what they have done, the sense of their learning self and of their capabilities is affirmed and transformed.

Environments for learning

When students arrive to study their course there are a number of firsts, and among the things they will do is to find the various rooms listed on their timetables and arrive punctually for their lectures, seminars, and workshops. Some courses will be an exception to this, if they involve remote delivery via a combination of synchronous and asynchronous communications or meetings across the Internet. However, the focus of most courses is the taught, regularly scheduled class session in a physical space on the campus (Smith & Valentine, 2012), whether it meets weekly, several times a week, or even intensively over several days.

Is this physical class space where the learning happens? Is it an appropriate environment for learning? Students come with expectations and learned skills and habits from years of previous schooling experiences. Wherever the space is where teachers find themselves, they need to find ways of working that allow for effective learning to take place. Students are repeatedly met with similar structures for learning as they move from one year to another in school, and within these there are traditional methods for teaching, with the teacher speaking and being supported by textbooks: lecturing is still a prevalent mode of delivery (Laurillard, 2013). Even the phrase 'mode of delivery' is riddled with associative meaning that is not always connected and certainly not interchangeable with learning. As an example, if 'mode of delivery' was replaced with 'mode of learning': *lecturing is the most prevalent mode of learning*, it would not make sense.

The lecture format still remains even though teachers are aware of the benefits of student-centred, active, problem-based learning, and there is a reluctance to change from established, traditional ways of presenting lectures as teaching (Weimer, 2013). Sometimes there is a lack of confidence, but also newer teachers can feel that they are not in a position to make significant changes if this involves the taught structure or assessment processes (Gibbs & Coffey, 2004). Lecturing does not guarantee learning, nor does it ensure that students develop and become more capable and confident in their pursuits. It is important to remember that the physical arch-shape lecture hall was designed by the Greeks not for learning, but as an arena with good acoustics that allowed spectators to view performance competitions (Smith & Anthon, 1843). Allowing a large number of students to see the speaker when the lecture hall was established fit within the world of higher education and the understanding at the time that students were passively receiving the master's knowledge (Jones, 2007). Lectures are generally passive happenings, described with words like 'sitting, watching, listening, telling', whereas learning is characterised with 'practice' meaning active engagement and performance (Mazur, 2014). Today, many institutions still boast having these facilities and label them as *learning* spaces, when they are actually *performing* spaces.

Environments for 'performing' assessments

> #### ...thinking about it
>
>   ▶ Where do you go for formal learning?
>   ▶ Does the understanding happen there in that place, or in quite a different setting?
>   ▶ As a teacher, where and when do you expect your students to learn?

Learning is an active process, something that people do, and students enter higher education to learn and prepare for their lives. Teachers work to give students the tools to develop skills, and throughout their studies various elements of knowledge and skill-base are tested. Sometimes students are asked to directly demonstrate practical understanding through an application where they have a chance to perform the specific tasks learned that contribute to their professional portfolio, but what if they are asked to sit for an exam or write an essay? There are many instances where it is not practical for a teacher to watch hundreds of students each individually carry out tasks. Written assessment is a commonplace method for asking students to communicate their understanding and evidence aspects of process through research and a written argument. An exam or an essay is still a performance, and as any assessment it comes with its own pressures.

There are elements of performance that transfer across learning contexts, and build on becoming a self-believing, autonomous learner. When a performer is successful and delivers a convincing performance, they are not only skilled, but display confidence and perhaps a flair for carrying out that task. Similar to a pianist on the stage, in an exam a student communicates about a given topic by calling on learned skills to articulate ideas and produce a final product in real time.

Considering academic work as a performance can encourage a shift in perspective. Once something is taken on board as a performance, it makes sense to prepare, and having a structure for building that confidence towards the achievement is likely to produce better results. Musical experts spend thousands of hours in the practice room, but they also practise all the aspects that bring the music from that private workshop room to the public arena of the concert hall. Students do perform through their assessments, and this is an opportunity to demonstrate learning and develop mastery experiences. Any learning space can be a performance space, but in order to prepare students, teachers must recognise what is being performed. Teachers can draw on this beyond the setting of final exams and essays, to consider how the assignments students complete throughout their studies can also become positive performed externalisations of their learning.

▶ Principles of excellence

The concept of excellence in higher education is not uniformly defined. Across the higher education sector there is a wide range of use and inclusion of the term 'excellence' in various rubrics, from subject benchmark statements to specific assessment criteria. Each metric uses specific terminology whether it is from an economic perspective, academic provision, facilities, student experience, excellence in learning, in teaching, in achievement; all have different orientations with respect to the terminology, and each definition is different depending on the institution, the context, and the subject.

It is interesting that when the term excellence is used in benchmarking statements, it is seldom with explicit contextual framework, terminology, or explanation. Although teachers would uniformly agree that excellence is something that is uniformly strived for, it does not feature or even appear in a single mention in the benchmark statements for all subject areas. There is no mention whatsoever of excellence in more than 30 of the 57 honours-subject benchmark statements published by the UK Quality Assurance Agency for Higher Education (QAA), and it is only mentioned notionally in several subject benchmark statements. For example, the only time excellence is mentioned in the English benchmark statement is to cite the increase in courses offered in the subject area as an 'excellent' demonstration of how the subject thrives (QAA, 2007a).

When excellence does appear as a descriptor, there is little explanation or context. The 'excellent student' is defined in the QAA benchmark for agriculture, horticulture, forestry, food and consumer sciences as a student who will 'have a range of competencies and skills at an enhanced level' (QAA, 2009, p.12). Theology provides a more specific descriptor of what this means: 'Excellent students transcend the learning outcomes and display originality, insight and the ability to progress to research' (QAA, 2014, p.21). Computing has an entire section on excellence and describes excellent students as 'creative and innovative in their application of the principles covered in the curriculum, and may relish the opportunity to engage in entrepreneurial activity' (QAA, 2007b, p.12).

The principles of excellence encompass going beyond requirements, beyond expectation, as students 'transcend the learning outcomes' (QAA, 2007c, p.9). Competence is assumed and innovation and creativity are requisite in achieving this.

> They will be able to act autonomously, demonstrate initiative, and demonstrate advanced problem-solving abilities. (QAA, 2008b, p.8)

Leaving space for this ambiguity can be challenging in both documentation and in practice, but it is important to recognise that the value of the pursuit of excellence, and indeed that it is a goal within the provision and processes of higher education.

> We have not attempted a characterisation of 'excellent' achievement. We confidently expect that excellent students will surprise us, will find ways of doing and saying things that we had not imagined. (QAA, 2008a, p.11)

These statements drawn from across subject areas, from agriculture, art and design, computing, dance, health studies, to theology, represent the subject areas where specific mention is given to excellence. The principles of excellence are not confined to any specific discipline or area of study, they transcend boundaries and are applicable to the essential qualities of the student, and these transpire as artefacts in the work these students produce.

Institutions represent excellence through marketing materials that use categorisation to highlight externally measurable aspects of the products of excellence, such as the ranking of the institution, the way student retention and completion are managed and maintained, and aspects of the student experience, such as contact time and curriculum structure (Ruben, 2007). However, this may be an exercise in optimising analysis of something that is subjective, as students cite the more humanistic qualities as defining qualities associated with excellence. The teachers and students who are directly involved in learning point out enthusiasm, creativity, and how teachers manage interpersonal relations as being essential signals of excellence (Hillier & Vielba, 2001; Hillier, 2002). Skelton (2005) stresses that these personalised aspects of excellence are often overlooked in an effort to officially document, and that it is essential to be aware and focus on the student and teacher perspectives. These voices can help teachers to notice and identify qualities of excellence, reflect on them, and see where there is room to explore and incorporate some of them in practical situations. They consider the scope of knowledge as part of excellence in their teachers, but also the integration of an awareness of effective communication, with smiles, humour, and a genuine interest in the students (Guardian Education, 2011). Schemes such as the student teaching awards that exist as student-driven projects at universities, as well as nationally based schemes, recognise individual teachers for excellence. Such schemes can single out and reward instances of excellence without designating a single model of excellence that is promoted, captured, and reproduced. There is no attempt to produce a template or encourage conformity. Excellence fosters the individual and allows for each to grow and develop their potential, as opposed to becoming a product of a predetermined process. It is important not to straightjacket practitioners into conforming to some expected model, as this would do exactly the opposite of nurturing the individual in teachers.

Excellent teaching

Teaching involves the students, their experience, and the interaction between all aspects of the curriculum, the space, and the people. The way students engage, from internal self-talk (Vygotsky, 1987), to activity in class, and across the wider context of their daily lives, is relevant to their learning and can be inspired and shaped by excellent teaching.

Those who are considered excellent teachers tend to have a broad concept of teaching, realising there is not only one approach to method or delivery (Dunkin & Precians, 1992). Teachers recognised for excellence tend to focus on a student-centred approach that encourages deeper understanding and aims to achieve a changed or transformed student perspective rather than working towards the direct transmission of knowledge (Salter & Lam Lai Ki, 2010). Reflective teaching that deals with problems through active engagement and is strongly student-centred leads to the understanding and adoption of a more encompassing approach. Surprisingly though, across subject areas teachers have been found to actively believe in the need to put the student and active learning at the centre of teaching, but when observed, practical teaching does not evidence this and instead demonstrates a more direct approach (Norton, Richardson, Heartley, Newstead, & Mayes, 2005).

Excellence in teaching does not mean invasive or overbearing teaching. Teachers who use student-centred approaches become sensitive to the teaching environment, anticipate and adapt as situations unfold, and allow their interactions with students to be shaped by the students' needs and the pace of their learning. It is not so radical to facilitate student thought and create genuinely meaningful experiences of learning that are relevant to the subject matter and meaningful to the students and their development. In the most stimulating settings, that encourage active, individual engagement, there is room for students to think, contribute to building content within the tasks or assessments, and to have sense of personal agency in their learning.

Teaching excellence to students

A teacher can be efficient and very skilled at communicating a factual base, but there are further elements to incorporate into the habit and process of learning if excellence is to be an outcome. Partly, this includes enabling achievement and leveraging towards success, but the qualities of going beyond and working deeper into understanding through experience involve more than the transmission of facts. The Boyer Commission (1999) produced a report containing an Academic Bill of Rights, and within its preamble stated that a college or university should provide 'maximal opportunities for intellectual and creative development' (p.12). The right listed as number one on the list is that students should have 'opportunities to learn through enquiry rather than simple transmission of knowledge' (p.12). Teachers who adopt a well-rounded approach that gives a variety of opportunities and allows for student integration have already taken a step towards teaching excellence to their students.

The expectation that goes with excellence, that students will create something surprising or of exceptional quality cannot be done without developing the required skills and demonstrating self-assuredness. Excellence cannot be measured by solely quantifiable means and includes elements that are uniquely personal. Outcomes cannot be achieved without belief, and in order to attain a level that is excellent students must refine their work, remain positive, and believe in both themselves and their capabilities. Teaching in a way that enables all of these qualities is far more complicated than guiding students through a textbook, and teaching the pattern of excellence is really about teaching a repeated and sustained practice of progressively building skill, awareness, confidence, achievement, and engaging with reflection that enables the student to continually refresh their perspective. Developing these qualities in students encompasses and involves both teaching and learning. When teachers communicate effectively, this involves having a clear message, and it also requires the student to be receptive, because communication requires an exchange. Teaching communication, and its importance, is often highlighted by the medical profession, as there is a direct use for communication with patients in the professional workplace. Deveugele et al. (2005) incorporated specific training in how to communicate within the curriculum for medical students, and after several years of developing the programme, they reported the importance and effectiveness of practice and rehearsal of these skills. Across professions and specialisms, students need to be encouraged that the communication of learning is a dialogue that involves them as much as it involves the input of the teacher. Developing each skill, quality, or attribute that relates to excellence requires dedicated development within the learning context.

Not only students, but also teachers need confidence and a sense of efficacy to be in a position where they can orient, carry out, and communicate their teaching in ways that encourage students to learn beyond the surface retention of facts. Teachers working to achieve this balance can adopt a student-centred approach that includes the technical detail, and also acknowledges the existence of individual factors that each student is subjectively involved with in learning. No teacher will ever, nor should they ever, know the details of every thought and reason that surrounds student learning, but understanding that there are individual and introspective aspects of learning that go beyond transmission, repetition, and reproduction of facts or skills is essential for leaving space for the learning process.

Learning is a holistic process and when aiming to teach students to attain the highest level of personal growth and academic achievement, teachers must allow space for thought, inquiry, and exploration within a learning environment that encourages awareness and reinforces progression. Gibbs and Coffey (2004) suggest that training is essential for teachers, and without a conscious reflection on practice there can be negative consequences where teachers become increasingly less effective at facilitating deep learning for their students. When teachers do take on board reflective practice, not only is their teaching more student-centred, but also the quality of student learning improves (Gibbs & Coffey, 2004, p.98).

Our students

Throughout education, students are taught a spectrum of academic and social skills, from reading and writing to how to work and play with others. The basic building blocks introducing how to listen, learn, question, perceive, understand, and retain the raw materials and information in the world surrounding these children are necessary and students will use them to take on board more complex concepts and begin to comprehend and explore as they progress through their learning. The initial years of schooling provide this valuable introduction and underpin the core skills and concepts that students will use throughout their lives in education.

However, when faced with deadlines and growing demands for constant grading, and pressures to demonstrate evidence of progress through results, children are schooled, at least to some extent, in providing the required answers on demand. Facts like times tables, spelling lists, and dates in history are memorised, and students learn how to demonstrate their knowledge on paper through tests and quizzes. When aiming for the right answers some of the freedom, independence, and autonomy that comes with play is not taken, but is schooled out of them. As children grow and develop, they also become increasingly aware of their surroundings, and social comparisons and hierarchies become an important part of the fabric of their lives. Comparing to those around you can have benefits, but it can also be incredibly limiting to students' self-perceptions and self-beliefs, and the impact depends on the situation and the ways learners engage within that peer group.

In America students aim for achieving a target score on college entry tests. A similar focus on testing and results exists in the UK, where students aged 14–15 choose classes for their GCSE exams which lead directly to their subsequent specialisation in the final two years of schooling as they prepare for A-level exams. In France, students prepare for the Baccalaureate exam before entry into higher education. Each country has its own approach, but testing is an inescapable part of education for children.

The shaping of students' perspectives is a delicate matter. In school there is a sense of striving and of moving forward through a structured progression that is laid out for students in the system. Textbooks have a next page, and the path of progression is made very clear: one step at a time. There is also often an expectation that students will be led and the teacher will tell them what to do (Newman, 2004), so after one assignment, students wait for the next task and then they complete that, to a deadline. This can create a culture where students believe that they can and should be passive while their teachers deliver education to them (Utley, 2004).

When students choose not to engage, because of an expectation that somehow education will happen 'to' them, it can undermine efforts by teachers to keep the student at the centre of learning (Little, Locke, Parker, & Richardson, 2007). This is highly ironic, because in higher education teachers aim to help prepare students for their professional lives, becoming independent, creative, confident thinkers. Sometimes there are students who are satisfied with a mere completion of the tasks at hand, and they do not engage more widely in their learning. For example, it is possible to tick the boxes of an assignment, by attending to assessment criteria, and not transferring learning or making connections with how the process and the experience of learning is a beneficial tool for them. Fortunately there are students at the other extreme of the spectrum who seem to magnetise themselves to every bit of information and manage to find relevance in every moment of their time both in and out of class.

▶ An ideal situation

An ideal situation looks forward with individual students as the centre of their own picture. McLuhan and Fiore (1967) suggest we, as a society, are 'rear-view' people, that there is a tendency to hold on to the familiar past and use it to label progress. The famous example in his book shows a picture of the rear-view mirror of a car, and in it is a picture of a horse-drawn carriage. The point being that the automobile was conceived of in terms of a horseless carriage, by relating it to the past instead of looking at it in a new context for what it was, meant, and could do. Although this controversial text is nearly half of a century old, there are still countless examples of this in everyday lives and in teaching and learning. There is value in retaining heritage through experience, but also a necessity to look forward with our students to their untrodden path. Taken from a completely different context, Dr Martin Luther King's words also transfer to the quest for independence and confidence in learning when he said: 'Take the first step in faith. You don't have to see the whole staircase, just take the first step' (Kuriansky, 2014).

In an ideal situation, students would have access to the raw materials that guide them to develop independence and become confident, autonomous thinkers. They would have support from teaching staff, access to information, and space in which to work. Crucially, students need permission to learn, think, and to engage with material in a way that encourages them to be positively active in ways beyond surviving a series of classes or lectures or sessions until an exam. Students need to overcome the barriers of insecurity or embarrassment when learning new material and working beyond their previous experience. Key to making educational experiences a part of a student's development as a person is the conscious awareness of the processes taking place internally, externally, collaboratively, with skills, application, and in various contexts.

Facilities

Whether flexible or static, a physical space can be either a help or hindrance to developing a sense of confidence and achievement in students. 'The Impact of School Environments' (Higgins, Hall, Wall,Woolner, & McCaughey, 2005), written for the UK Design Council, points out that too much ambient noise or poor circulation in a space can have negative impacts on all within the learning environment (p.6). There are of course other aspects of facilities and a learning environment that can be extremely beneficial to all, and many teachers use their teaching spaces distinctly as an asset to student learning. For example, Professor Clive Holtham, National Teaching Fellow, adopted the concept of 'priority seating' for his business studies students in London. He purchased a number of comfy sofas that are available to the students who arrive to class first, instead of the typical, less comfortable classroom chairs, thereby encouraging punctuality and acting as a token reward and outward sign of recognition for those students who arrive early.

Associate Professor of Architecture Mark Cabrinha allowed his students at Cal Poly to redesign their learning space in the way that they felt it would best suit their learning.

Case study 1.1: Redesigning learning spaces

Students created something that resembled a long rectangular family or kitchen table and placed this in the centre of the room, with individual student desks at the periphery of the space. This table became the hub for class discussions while desks at the periphery allowed for individual work. As a studio environment, common in design, art, and architecture education, emphasis is placed on individual work with instruction based on individual critique or 'desk-crits'. The introduction of this family table altered the social dynamic of the space: it became a social hub for studio presentations and discussions, it allowed for informal small group discussion with the teacher while other students not part of this discussion could still hear and observe what was being discussed while they developed their individual work, and most surprisingly, it became a literal family table for numerous potluck-type meals inspired by the students. Rather than sitting at a conference table at the corner of the room as Professor Cabrinha did previously, the students' choice to place the teacher at the centre of the room made the teacher more approachable, while allowing other students engaged with their individual work to listen in at the periphery.

Giving these students the opportunity to 'hack' their learning environment not only created a new focal element at the centre of the room, but this became a powerful tool that altered the social dynamic and productive energy in this active learning environment.

As teachers though, there needs to be a consideration for the physical tools that are available for students, so a lack of provision does not present a barrier to engagement. Neither musicians nor doctors can learn to practise without instruments and appropriate spaces. Equity of provision is a topic that differs with reference to different subject areas. Sometimes facilities are necessary and incredibly important, but equipment alone does not necessitate that learning will take place. There are instances when a plain room with four bare walls is the only physical requirement for learning. It is about perspective. Facilities and materials can be leveraged to encourage engagement and enable the best outcome for students. Martin, Katz, Morris, and Kilgallon (2008) include three types of spaces in their discussion of learning: the physical, virtual, and personal spaces.

Case study 1.2: Using spaces creatively to facilitate attention and engagement

In the space of one lecture I took part in at Coventry University, the room seemed to bend particularly well to the changing needs of the students.

The pseudo-amphitheatre had unexpected modifications. The raked seating was in the form of three large terraced levels, each more resembling something built out of giant one-metre Lego blocks, and completely unlike typical furnishings in a university lecture space. To make this terrace more appealing, it was completely covered with a plush carpet of long artificial grass. The space was framed with a tall wooden wall that did not reach to the ceiling, but remained open with the rest of the giant, multipurpose open-plan floor in the Disruptive Media Learning Laboratory space. A number of staff and 30 students were present, and the session began with an interactive trans-media workshop that included an orchestra of instruments (none of the students were either studying music or were musicians; this was an exercise in teamwork), and so every person on the terrace was actively involved in the session and attention was jointly divided between their own activities, their peers around them, and the leader seated at the front and centre of the semicircle. The session continued with a discussion led by staff who were sitting among the students on the terrace, and this brought attention inward, and then with the inclusion of a Skype connection, all attention was diverted to a large screen on the wall. Finally the focus shifted to individual students, as each presented their final project work. The space created a flow between activities and learning; the shift of focus from students to teachers, and from the centre to the group, was a powerful demonstration of how a shell of a room could be inviting, as opposed to a limitation. The combination of using the student's personal and mental space in conjunction with the physical space allowed for a truly exciting session.

Liberating the concept of the teaching and learning facility to include spaces beyond the current physical setting may feel like a difficult leap for some. As teachers are already stretched with working hours, the idea of structured learning that extended without end would be far too much. However, students do not stop learning when the clock strikes the hour and class is finished, and if there is a way to allow for this continued learning outside the physical space, then there are new possibilities. There has always been the expectation that students do homework and study outside of class. What about out of class application? The best plans for teaching and learning excellence call for active participation.

Technology is a part of students' lives full stop. There is a false sense in education that this is something to be adopted by teachers to be innovative. Today it is impossible for teachers to be ahead of any technological development, and it is a big challenge just to be apprised of the latest innovations in any one field. It is important that technology is used in learning in ways that complement its use in students' everyday lives: students are already connected. Using different means of technology is not about integrating something 'new' into the curriculum, but joining in with what is already in practice. That is a difficult concept for many teachers, as it may genuinely be new for them, whereas for the students it is the norm. They have always known social media and apps, and it is up to the teacher to choose what is most useful for the learning purposes within that coursework. With any choice, from an internal learning management system like Moodle or Blackboard to syndicating and commenting on external blog posts, or any device there needs to be enough uptake within the teaching setting that the platform or tool works and becomes a part of the normal discourse between students and teachers within that class.

The current generation of teachers has a valuable and irreplaceable insight into the experience of learning without the current technologies. For example, the students know what they can do with their smartphones, and they have grown up with personal experience of this technology in their lives. Today's teachers, on the other hand, can draw on the experience of not having had such technology yesterday, and reflect on the changes that they see. Their experience is unique from the students and allows them to reflect on and understand what technology might mean as opposed to just what it does. So if the motor car was invented today, one would expect an instructor to provide instruction on how to drive, but hope the teacher might also realise the wider implications and teach the student about the employability and market economy of malls, effects of obesity and exercise, and global warming. It is the teacher's duty to explore the possible meanings with students so they can be mindful and develop agency. It is about learning and understanding why and how it affects the processes taking place and what it means. With this understanding, the student can be enabled to understand, synthesise meaning, and learn: by taking responsibility, having purpose, and believing in their actions, students ultimately will be in a position to shape the technologies they use instead of allowing technology to shape them (Worth, 2014a).

Without this outlook, the empowerment of having information at students fingertips is false, as they are not being empowered to creatively use their own agency; instead, they are looking in what appears to be a wider source pool, but is in fact either what someone else thinks the student wants to see or what it is believed the student *should* see. Practical examples include the limitations of the tailored results from search engines that harvest information and present biased user information, based on previous searching. The bias there is of the user, reflected back to the student, and this makes it increasingly less likely that the student will actually discover anything new. An example of this on a different platform is that Twitter will present suggestions reflecting the user's bias. Here the user is likely to follow people they agree with, and although the user perceives they are having a clear view of the world, in fact it is very limited and basically self-confirmatory. When using a search engine, where information is presented via a curated list, there are different limiting biases presented. In this setting the list could be compiled, for example, by someone with a dislike of Shakespeare, and as a result, the student searching for information may never discover Shakespeare because of the curator's bias. The information presented here demonstrates the preferences of somebody else. This also happens as in adaptive learning where information that is deemed most suitable is presented to the student (Ruiz, Mintzer, & Leipzig, 2006). In learning, whether with physical space, information and technology, or the personal arena, it is important to know what the facilities are and how they can be used to open doors to student creativity and development.

Tailored programmes

Having open access to information and carte blanche to create something specifically for that person is too much for all but a very few individuals. Students need structure and guidance in their learning, especially when delving into subject matter at the tertiary level. Curricula based solely on delivering the content will easily give guidelines that give students the parameters for their work, but as this design is not ideal for developing the whole student, there need to be adaptions. When broadening the experience and including different formats of interactions with content and the wider learning community, students can be reluctant to engage with what is new if it is perceived to be overly difficult or if it threatens their sense of security. It is a risk for students, as they need to personally invest themselves in what they are doing, and what seems to be outside the direct assessment box may be seen as extra and irrelevant. Students have challenges in learning, with the investment of time and their personal energies. If they have something presented to them, especially if it is additional and not for credit towards their grade, they need to know how it is relevant and how it relates to their lives. In order to give students a sense of security, purpose, and comfort, teachers can give guide processes, showing students the why. Bresnahan (2012) suggests, 'Announce that you're an accommodationist.' The outward act of telling students that tasks are relevant, and that they can expect involvement from the teacher to assist their learning across activities and processes, opens the doors to clear communication. It removes the mystery surrounding expectations about student participation and makes clear that the learning is about the student, and happens collaboratively, with the mentorship of the teacher.

Jonathan Worth, National Teaching Fellow, took over the teaching of a final year undergraduate photography module at Coventry University where students prepared an exhibition as their assessed coursework. He devised the course as an entirely interest-driven learning experience. In the first of the ten-week sessions, students were asked *what would they like* in the course. This open-ended question allowed students to have a direct input into building their experiences. The responses illustrated a real need for including development beyond content, to include their self-beliefs and a desire to connect with their future in the profession. The students asked for a series of interviews, and a tutorial-led programme, where each lecture session would be based around bespoke talks. To direct the learning, each student would have specific assigned tasks that were tailored to them, and the tutorials would be based on helping students work towards completing their tasks. For example, the student who wanted to pursue wedding photography would have a different task than someone interested in becoming an archivist, and the photojournalist would have yet another task. In essence, each of the students was able to carve a personalised route for their learning in that module, instead of having a prescriptive situation where everyone produces a version of the same task. With this level of diversity, there needed to be a common goal to unify the students. The photography class as a whole shared a vision that each person's pursuit embodied an 'exit strategy'; their goal went beyond the physical assessment material and related to their lives. An exhibition alone was not seen as the best way to allocate teaching resources or student energies when considering the longer-term view and development of the whole student, beyond a single skill set.

If a goal is to prepare students to engage with industry, or to prepare them for a professional life, there needs to be a different perspective through the course process. The assessment artefact – a photograph, an essay, or an exam – is not sufficient as the main focus of the learning, because it reinforces a culture that is essentially about ticking boxes to gain points, and less about the overall learning of the student. In Jonathan Worth's photography class, the variety infused into the course by the student input meant that much of the work produced was 'unhitched from time and space, online' (Worth, 2014a). It still was represented in a physical form for the students' exhibition, but there was a larger purpose, and students oriented the presentation and position of their work in a globally facing way. (See discussion in Chapter 7 on *Hashtag Magazine*.)

The classroom setting is a generative experience (Kelly, 2008) and is an essential part of the higher education experience. Allowing students a voice in tailoring their course encourages them to look beyond any minimal require-ments, and means that they have a reason to be genuinely motivated to spend the time and effort on what may have otherwise seemed like peripheral tasks within a class. The role of the teacher then is not simply a 'one to many' dispenser of information. The technologically connected classroom is infor-mation rich, but information and meaning seldom come bundled together. The teacher's role becomes to curate and contextualise this information. Teachers are librarians, who are already themselves the key to the under-standing of all the information in the library. Without this person, the library is a room full of paper, but the teacher can lead each student by the hand to edit, curate, and contextualise a journey through this information so that meaning can be created (Worth, 2014b). When thinking like this, it connects the teacher both to the students and integrally to the teaching and learning processes. When students find meaning, they find confidence and begin to gain personal power and agency to leverage their work in a wider context. They too begin to curate and edit information. When the student experience is at the centre of the teaching, they can each personally develop a sense of agency and their capabilities in ways that empower them and reinforces their self-beliefs through the teaching and learning experiences.

Mutual engagement

A didactic teaching approach can leave the teacher as a spectator after pro-viding the initial fodder or catalyst for learning. Having a purely hierarchi-cal system that originates from the teacher creates a barrier for the student and stops the flow of learning. Ito (2010) suggests that horizontal networks encourage feedback and reciprocity, and that in assessment-driven settings students orient themselves to that external framework, whereas in peer-inclusive settings their reputation and system of values unfolds organically. Neary and Winn (2009) reinforce the strength in reciprocity, explaining that when an approach of mutual engagement is adopted,

> the organizing principle is being redressed creating a teaching, learning and research environment which promotes the values of openness and creativity, engenders equity among academics and students and thereby offers an opportunity to reconstruct the student as producer and academic as collaborator. The educator is no longer a delivery vehicle (p.138)

With this openness, there is a commonality and community of experience that allows for the student to direct and own their development. If the teacher is an active mentor and contributor (but not dictator) in guiding, shaping, and integrating experiences, then the learning process will not be something that is presented on a tray for the student to take away and digest. Fostering students' self-beliefs in their confidence and capabilities is built on an investment and connection with students' journeys as they explore and develop their learning and performing processes through skills, goals, and experiences.

2 Whole students

The concept of self-efficacy is examined in detail, considering specifically how it is influenced and formed. These beliefs are oriented within the student's overall perception of their 'self' and contextualised within learning and achieving in a higher education setting. The overall importance and relevance of developing self-efficacy beliefs is presented and the chapter begins introducing how to bring these concepts to a practical teaching setting.

Teaching is a complicated mixture of different elements within any discipline, from the core curriculum and skills development to the understanding of concepts, facts, and a historical context, that all lead towards a practical application within the discipline. These could be considered in a pure or theoretical manner, with an outline of the content, or a diagram representing technical information, but this does not allow for the complexities of interaction within the teaching situation. In reality, teaching involves communication between people who have their own thoughts and must make choices that lead to the actions they pursue. Each student brings his or her own unique dynamic to a situation, with a microcosm of personal attributes, beliefs, and experiences the teacher may never see.

The psychologist Albert Bandura (1986) divides the web of everyday human interaction into three components that impact one another: *personal influences* interact with *environmental influences* and lead people to make *behavioural choices* (Figure 2.1).

People's behaviours or actions then complete the cycle and influence the next situation, shaping future activities and contexts. Within this reciprocal framework, as set out in *Social Foundations in Thought and Action* (Bandura, 1986), individuals have control over their own thoughts, emotions, and behaviour, and it is their personal beliefs that link knowledge, or thought, and action. Within the teaching context, students interact within the framework of learning consisting of themselves, their thoughts and beliefs (personal influences), the teacher, the content, and the learning space (environmental influences), and their actions (behavioural choices). Specific self-efficacy beliefs, a person's beliefs about their capabilities to accomplish a specific, criterial task (Bandura, 1977), are the focus of this chapter. These beliefs are entwined in all three elements of this model of human interaction, and are relevant to learning methods, commitment, and engagement, and ultimately affect achievement.

Effective teaching is meaningful for students, and makes a connection with them. People affect one another, and talking and thinking and listening

HARROW COLLEGE
Learning Centre

Figure 2.1 Web of everyday interaction

and doing all contribute to building knowledge and experience. From the first impression of the class and teaching room, the student is flooded with thoughts and perceptions that affect their learning and performing, either positively with eagerness or perhaps with anticipation or worry. The internal influences and processes that affect the students, teachers, and the learning dynamic are explored in this chapter.

It can be hugely challenging when considering the complex interaction of everything in the teaching situation, from the teacher, methods, and material, to still allowing for the student to also be an individual, with their own ambition, understanding, and accomplishments. Allowing for individuals certainly does not mean probing students' personal lives to understand their perspectives. However, it is important to acknowledge that the student's decisions, thinking, motivation, and achievements are based on a multifaceted web of self-beliefs. Self-efficacy beliefs are, by definition, specific to a named task, and that means that there will be self-efficacy beliefs that are directly related to the teaching context. Moreover, these beliefs are malleable, and we as teachers can influence how they are formed and maintained. An understanding of self-efficacy beliefs can greatly inform the methods and approach used in teaching. Considering individuals and what they bring to learning can transform both learning and teaching.

▶ Self-efficacy and 'the self'

Students' self-views encompass many different aspects of their lives, including experiences with learning, influences, and interactions within the teaching space. Other views or beliefs may be purely personal or socially based and may never have a place within the lecture hall or classroom. Self-concept originates from a complex mixture of influences that combine external and internal factors (Bong & Clark, 1999). It is a composite understanding that includes comparisons with social norms, feelings of worth and value, and judgements based on various relationships (Bandura, 1993, 2006; Pajares, 1996b).

A teacher will gain an understanding of a student's self-concept through his or her attitude, demeanour, and everyday interactions with others. As a general or holistic self-belief, self-concept goes with a student to permeate different contexts or settings. For example, someone may ask, 'Do you know a person in the first year called Eve?' and receive the reply, 'Ah yes, she's the eager student with a sunny disposition', or 'Oh, she's terribly grumpy and always worried about something.' These descriptions are evidence of the generality associated with an overall self-concept. A person's understanding of his or her value as an individual is separate from the self-efficacy beliefs based on capabilities to carry out named tasks. Even with a very strong or positive self-concept, someone might not be so confident when it comes to working or learning within a given subject area. Someone may have a good self-concept and believe that they are a valid person, but when it comes to beliefs about successfully taking a high dive, or preparing a soufflé, confidence levels might be quite different. A student's overall self-concept is a global trait, and as such, is less relevant to any specific teaching context.

In contrast, self-efficacy beliefs are not generalised views, but are always specific within a given context (Pajares, 1996a; Schunk, 1996a; Bandura, 2006). These task-specific beliefs are formulated solely from internal self-judgements and do not use external socially based comparisons. Self-efficacy beliefs are not qualified, categorised, or tied to an external, predetermined grading system. To judge self-efficacy beliefs a person looks inside and asks, 'How confident am I that I can do this (specific task)?' and the answer is based upon different factors involving his or her experience and understanding at that moment.

When people attempt to judge themselves against peers or other social markers instead of using self-judgements, it is a sign of more naïve learners who are dependent on proximal, immediate means to monitor and quantify their progress. Social comparison is not the basis on which mature learners form their self-efficacy beliefs (Zimmerman & Martinez-Pons, 1988; Schunk, 1996b). Pajares (1996b, p.563) explained that although self-efficacy and self-concept (Eccles, Adler, & Meece, 1984) are often related, self-efficacy beliefs informed the wider self-concept, and it is possible to have a high self-efficacy for carrying out a certain task while taking no pride in the task, therefore having little or no contribution to that person's self-concept.

▶ Research into self-efficacy

Self-efficacy views are personal, and by nature that means that they are largely unseen. Research studies are valuable as they quantify and expose various aspects of what people think and feel, and relate these private beliefs to external actions. Self-efficacy beliefs are pivotal to choices, effort, and success, and the findings of formalised research studies help to pinpoint and demonstrate both what self-efficacy is and why it matters in practical settings. There are many more studies across diverse disciplines than are mentioned in this chapter, as this discussion is mainly limited to studies within educational settings.

Self-efficacy was first studied by Bandura in the 1970s within the context of psychotherapy. Bandura's initial study (1977) involved a group of patients being treated for a phobia of snakes. Individuals' beliefs were measured for their confidence in their capabilities to carry out progressive tasks involving boa constrictors: being in the same room as the snake, touching the snake, holding the snake. Each person had a unique and personal belief about their capabilities to do the different tasks based on self-judgements made at that point in time. The study illustrated the differentiation of self-efficacy beliefs from one task to another and how the strength of people's beliefs impacted their achievements. Self-efficacy beliefs can change over time, in different settings, and as people gain experience with tasks. These beliefs can be shaped and influenced by teachers through the learning and teaching process.

Self-efficacy beliefs are not simply determined by attaining a certain skill level, but are influenced by several factors. Within educational settings, several studies have examined school children's self-efficacy beliefs with reference to subject areas, such as social studies (Zimmerman & Martinez-Pons, 1988), English (Shell, Murphy, & Bruning, 1989; Zimmerman, Bandura, & Martinez-Pons, 1992; Schunk & Rice, 1993), psychology (Greene & Miller, 1996), music (McPherson & McCormick, 2006; Ritchie &

Williamon, 2012), and mathematics (Zimmerman & Martinez-Pons, 1990; Konstantopolous, 1996). Explorations into student's self-efficacy are typically very specific to a context, because the beliefs themselves are tied to the task at hand. So when studying self-efficacy beliefs for repeatedly achieving an accurate high dive (as in Feltz, Chow, & Hepler, 2006), there are some aspects of that research that relate only to that discipline and cannot be transferred even beyond that specific task.

There has not been a definitive way to represent or measure self-efficacy within a subject, but it has been recognised as being a very important self-belief that affects learning and performance. The body of research on self-efficacy is substantive, but as the beliefs are specific, results are also specific, and not automatically generalisable to any subject. Where there are active researchers there are good sources of information on the topic; however, there are also unfortunately disciplines that remain untouched, such as dance, and this leaves a real gap in published research. The problem is that a generalised study tends to miss the mark and measure self-concept or a more generalised view rather than the very specific self-efficacy beliefs.

Educational investigations have explored student's self-efficacy in relation to the outcomes of assessments and courses, and they have questioned how these beliefs fit into a larger picture of the self. Different methods of questioning have been trailed and tested in experimental settings. In the past, a few researchers have adopted a very specific approach to measuring self-efficacy that goes beyond a questionnaire about the different aspects of beliefs for completing that task. In mathematics research, students have been presented with actual sample problems, just to view, and then asked about their self-efficacy to solve very similar problems, thus ensuring that the measurement corresponded to a task (Schunk, 1981; see also Schunk, 1996a). This also ensured that the students all conceived of exactly the same task, avoiding any misinterpretation of contexts. The suggestion is not for every teacher to conduct research studies, but to be aware of the construct and of how the elements of self-efficacy are relevant to both teachers and students. Without the detailed approach from researchers and an explanation of the usefulness of results, the understanding and benefits of self-efficacy may remain unexplored by practising teachers and lecturers.

▶ Sources and influences

Looking at self-efficacy beliefs is like viewing snapshots of people's self-judgement of their confidence in capabilities in that moment. They are based on a number of different experiences and factors revolving around the task at hand, involving that person and their environment, actions and observations, and thoughts and reflections. Especially when students study something that is new to them, it is a teacher's privilege and responsibility to guide learning. By creating a framework of positive experiences, beliefs will build and enable each student to approach new tasks with confidence and security. Decades of research have reinforced aspects of the four main methods of forming and influencing self-efficacy beliefs that were first outlined by Bandura (1986): mastery experiences, vicarious experiences, verbal persuasion, and physical signals. These influences are listed in order of importance. Considering the nature of self-efficacy beliefs is incredibly important, as without a foundation for a personal belief in capabilities, or worse yet, with negative self-judgements, some students might not even begin to engage with tasks.

Mastery experiences

The most meaningful and lasting way to impact self-efficacy beliefs is through personal experiences. When someone takes on a task and completes it, they achieve what is called a *mastery experience* (Zimmerman, 2000; Bandura, 2006). This can be on any level, so a student could master conversational French, or successfully learn to conjugate a single verb. Each task, whether micro or macro, can represent a mastery experience. These accomplishments inform future beliefs in capabilities to carry out similar tasks. The gravity of this becomes clear when considering how students learn new material. Their first experiences, whether positive or negative, will form the foundation for self-efficacy beliefs, and this impacts the approach and success of new endeavours.

Consider when a student is met with something new, perhaps there is some lab work that is being introduced as follow-up work for a lecture. Before they have actually done the task they do not know for certain how success-fully they will carry out the task. When the student asks, 'Can I do this?' the honest answer could be, 'I'm not sure.' Sometimes there is no direct experi-ence on which the student could base a confident judgement, and therefore their initial self-efficacy beliefs for the completing of that new lab work might be quite weak.

Even when students have no direct experience with a task, their beliefs are still based on something, even if the grounds for belief may be only tangen-tially connected to the task. For example, in a study of primary school chil-dren's first introduction to learning musical instruments (Ritchie & Williamon, 2011), the children had very little specific musical knowledge at the outset of the programme, and the children still made judgements about their self-efficacy beliefs for learning to play the instruments. In the absence of any specific musical experience, or prior engagement with the task, their beliefs were based on ideas about other tasks that they imagined to be similar. For some children they equated learning an instrument with playing individual sports, and others associated music learning with independent reading. On a simple level this can be seen in the way that one child spoke about the instrument he was learning. The little boy reported that he was going to learn the 'elbow', as when he heard 'oboe', which he had never seen or heard of before, he mentally replaced it with something he did understand. A student's first mastery experience is one of the most important building blocks of their self-efficacy beliefs. With carefully planned and presented activities, teachers can guide students through assignments and accomplishments so they create a foundation for positive self-efficacy beliefs. Wayne et al. (2006) describe integrating simulators to facilitate realistic mastery experiences for medical students training in America as they study for their advanced cardiac life support accreditation. Approximating real-life situations links the study to the practice and ensures that students are as prepared as possible for various possibilities.

Vicarious experiences

A learner has a *vicarious experience* when observing others accomplish tasks, and this can influence their self-efficacy beliefs (Schunk, 1998). Vicarious learning is commonplace in academic settings, and students are often asked to observe teachers or peers. For example, sports students will see others who have already mastered tasks perform at a high level in competitions and public events. When students watch, they can compare themselves to the competitor on the track or pitch. This comparison can affect self-perception on many different levels. If a female student watches another woman perform a floor routine in gymnastics, she may compare their ages, body build, perhaps analyse the core skills involved in the routine, speculating whether her own training or skill level is comparable to the competitor, and similar comparisons will happen across subject areas with the student and the person modelling or performing the activity (Schunk, 2003). This experience impacts beliefs and allows a more informed self-efficacy judgement, and sense of how well 'can I do it'. Of course, if the observer has also taken part in the activity, and has their own mastery experiences, then their personal experience will be more influential than what is observed in others.

Self-efficacy can be influenced by watching professionals demonstrate mastery, and it can also be built and reinforced when watching someone less experienced who is working through the difficulties towards completing a task (Schunk, 1998). Peers who observe each other coping with new skills and managing the situation imagine being in that situation, and working towards the goal. Vicarious learning can be effective when introducing completely new material or when rebuilding students after less than successful experiences. If a student has perhaps failed at a task, which could be because of rushing through instructions, being ill prepared, or having a bit of bad luck on the day, then seeing the steps worked out in a positive way can help them to overcome the negative experience and rebuild their self-efficacy for the next time they encounter the situation. When a student is asked to demonstrate something to the class, or to reply to questions, often this involves trial and error, and observers can learn from the processes observed. Watching others can communicate a sense that the task is possible, as they know someone else has achieved it.

There are countless possibilities for incorporating this into a classroom setting. From a teaching point of view, the requisite steps for completing a task need to be understood and prepared for the students to follow so they can then literally be in a position to retrace their path and reflect upon the progress that led to their achievement. Besides observing others, students can also practice self-reflection to observe themselves, and this combination of having an end goal and reflecting on progress builds self-efficacy beliefs (Schunk, 1996b). In a guided task or group work situation, an element of reflection can be embedded within the task, so students are noting the underlying methods, skills, and processes as they progress through the different stages of the assignment. Any modelled experience can be banked, along with their experiences, to help prepare them for the next situation.

Verbal persuasion and feedback

To a lesser extent, self-efficacy beliefs are influenced through verbal persuasion, feedback, or encouragement (Jordan, 1992). None of the influences are as strong as actually experiencing the success or failure of doing something in person, and a mastery experience will supersede both observations and what other people say in encouragement. Verbal persuasion alone is not an effective way to form or influence self-efficacy beliefs, and the effects of verbal feedback tend to be temporary. Verbal persuasion is more effective when it is followed by an accomplishment (Bouffard-Bouchard, 1990). For example, if students are simply told that they can achieve something, the influence will be minimal, but if they then do it the advice will have a far greater impact on their self-efficacy beliefs.

The more experienced students are, the less they will simply trust advice from a teacher or mentor without supporting experience. Imagine if a drama coach said 'you'll be fine on stage', the dentist to his student, 'I'm sure the drilling will go well', or for a more common occurrence, a teacher said to a student, 'you can write a good essay'. These are valuable words to hear, but it would be unheard of to simply tell someone that they will be fine when they lacked the requisite skills and experience. This is why teachers model, build mock situations, and create many preliminary experiences before putting students in more high-pressured settings. The words given in encouragement are still important and will make an impression on students, but care must be taken, as the effect of the carrying out the task may supersede the verbal persuasion (Greenlees, Nunn, Graydon, & Maynard, 1999). If success is promised but failure results, the act of failing will override the encouragement and this could have a far more damaging impact than not saying anything at all. However, if the student succeeds, this will reinforce the teacher's words.

In educational settings, no matter how well-planned the curriculum or how skilled the teacher is at encouraging students to take their own path, socially based comparisons with other classmates and their marks or grades are unavoidable. Students will be aware of who achieved top marks and who struggled, and this dynamic is present to various degrees within teaching environments. When social comments arise, these can be unplanned forms of verbal persuasion, and they can and will affect self-efficacy beliefs, especially of those who view their intelligence as unchangeable. There is a vast difference between believing in fixed abilities or in capabilities (Bandura & Dweck, 1988). 'Are you able?' is a yes or no question, whereas a student may not be able to do something right now but can have the capability to achieve something in the future. Capabilities are boundless and can be developed over time, whereas abilities can have a fixed ceiling that puts limits on students.

The influences of self-efficacy need to be carefully considered in academic settings, where students often put themselves in the vulnerable position of learning new things and being shaped by new experiences. It is important that teachers realise the persuasive role of feedback and its impact on self-efficacy: feedback can be presented in a way that encourages the student to strive further, or merely to recognise failure. A focus on achieved progress keeps the attention on the learner's capabilities, whereas focusing on errors will point out the student's weaknesses. Teachers can facilitate the positive development of solid self-efficacy beliefs. Learning and feedback that treat ability as an acquirable skill use self-comparisons instead of requiring a social framework, and focus on the self and achieved progress has been recommended for building self-efficacy (Jordan, 1992).

Physical signals

Finally, the actual physical state of the student will influence self-efficacy. These beliefs do change, and even if someone has mastered the situation before, it is very possible that on a different occasion they *feel* differently. They may become nervous, or perhaps time was short and they forgot to eat well or to drink enough water on a hot day before entering the exam room. Physiological signs such as a dry mouth, sweaty palms, tiredness, or stress may also affect a person's belief in his or her capabilities to carry out a task (Schunk, 1996a). This is the least influential factor on a person's self-efficacy beliefs, and positive influences from mastery or vicarious experiences can override the butterflies of nervousness and carry a student through an experience.

Without a successful track record of experiences, this lesser influence of how people feel on the day and the input or feedback from others both become more important to self-efficacy judgements. This can happen when a great deal of technical information needs to be communicated and there may not be the practical experience to compliment it. Consider trainee teachers, who learn about the theory and study classroom dynamics before they enter the live situation for the first time. The theory taught in class may be the closest that some students have to handling a class of children until they experience it first-hand. In a less dramatic fashion, students are often taught practical concepts that they are expected to demonstrate through writing in assessment settings. An essay or exam may require students to verbally describe a process or procedure, and the student may not have experience with writing about practical processes. Some programmes have an end-of-year assessment, but do the students undertake similar assessment-like experiences to prepare them for it, or is the first time also the only time they encounter that specific task? Students are provided with a strong starting point to achieve positive experiences when contexts are clear, accomplishment is recognised, and each student is allowed to enter situations with their own unique perspective.

▶ Impacts and implications

Self-efficacy is integral to the learning and teaching process and to everyday functioning. People who have high levels of self-efficacy also tend to exhibit a range of positive qualities. They are more likely to choose more challenging tasks, undertake strategic thinking, work harder, exhibit resilience, and attain higher outcomes (Zimmerman, 2000). In the face of challenges, they are more likely to think through, find, and follow a progressive, hierarchical path to reach their goals. Failure is less of a deterrent for these people, and they use resources creatively and seek possible solutions before giving up. Overall they persist longer and achieve more. Self-efficacy is a personal belief, but it affects the choice of task, the effort committed, and outcomes achieved. It is a belief worth cultivating in our students.

Ability or capability?

Self-efficacy beliefs are partly informed by people's understanding of their ability (Schunk, 1996b), which can be either as a trait that is inherited and unchangeable, or as a skill that can be acquired and developed over time (Bandura & Dweck, 1988). When given the same directions and task, individual students can produce completely divergent responses. One student may fully engage and relish all that the task has to offer, whereas another may shy away and purposefully avoid challenges. People are complex, with their own attributes and unique beliefs about themselves and their capabilities. Some are confident, whereas others doubt themselves. There will be varying levels of prior experience and/or success with the subject matter, and engaging in a public setting like a lecture or seminar can seem scary and potentially exposing for students, especially if they are unsure of themselves. Collins (1982) illustrated exactly these differences with a sample of mathematics students who all had similar abilities levels. Though in the same class, the students in the study had different levels of self-efficacy beliefs for completing the set work. Those who had higher self-efficacy achieved higher results on examinations, despite having comparable ability levels. This study demonstrated that having the requisite knowledge was not enough to ensure the student would achieve, but that accomplishments required both skill and belief, especially in a challenging situation.

Self-efficacy impacts choices, and for those who consider their abilities to be predetermined, performance has negative connotations as it is an opportunity for them to face what they believe to be their limitations and threaten any positive self-beliefs they do hold. Because of this, such people will avoid a challenging situation so they are not in a position to make errors or to look bad in the face of their peers. These people often have lower self-efficacy and need guidance to realise that they do have the capability to achieve. It is possible to break through the mindset that someone *can't* learn by demonstrating to them that they *have* already learned. In effect, the teacher can walk students through their learning and be a sort of commentator throughout the processes, verbally acting out the process of reflection for the student. This way, the student becomes aware of having achieved mastery, and the experience gained with the teacher's help will serve to build the belief that he or she can learn.

Those who believe they are capable of increasing their ability levels as they pursue challenges and work towards mastery tend to have more solid self-efficacy beliefs. They will continuously make and refine judgements about their ability in reference to personal progress and accomplishment, rather than relying on external frameworks as diagnostic tools. The processes of reflecting and reassessing help self-efficacious people to take on more challenging tasks with continued confidence; they focus strategically on how to use their skills to achieve success.

Impact on behaviour

Self-beliefs are associated with positive personal qualities and attributes. Exploring the different facets of a situation and analysing the factors involved can highlight relationships between physical actions, thoughts or beliefs, methods, and the resulting outcomes. Consciously acknowledging these relationships, and paying attention to patterns of experience, allows individuals to form a mental map of how these beliefs affect learning and performing processes for them. The qualities associated with self-efficacy can be contextualised by situating them both within Bandura's (1986) model for human functioning involving the personal, environmental, and behavioural aspects of a situation, and aligning these beliefs with self-processes involved within learning (Zimmerman et al., 1992). These can be either understood on either a large- or small-scale level.

A student may come to the first session of a class with the personal view that it is going to be boring and difficult; it is a new subject area and he or she has no prior experience within this area. As a result they have a very low self-efficacy for engaging with that class, and an even lower self-efficacy for carrying out the required assessment tasks. However, the teacher then enters, full of enthusiasm, and presents the first session with clarity and somehow makes it appealing as opposed to daunting.

The interaction between the initial personal beliefs and expectations and the environmental factors will have an impact on the students' perceived self-efficacy and influences their behavioural decisions. For example, committing to a goal is partly determined by self-efficacy, and the actions that follow are also sustained by these beliefs, and lead to achievements, which are the basis for future judgements about self-efficacy. The framework for human functioning of personal, behavioural, and environmental factors is relevant to practical applications of the influences, effects, and relationships of self-efficacy beliefs to students' choices. The whole process is a cycle that feeds back into itself.

Within the learning process

'One cannot conjure up outcomes without giving thought to what one is doing and how well one is doing it' (Bandura, 1984, p.232). This thought happens within learning when people plan and consider the actions and approach they will take. As Bandura (1984) explains, 'human causal thinking places actions before the outcomes that flow from them' (p.237).

Considering the microscopic level, students learn to implement new concepts and skills through individual assignments. Self-efficacy beliefs are assessed at the outset of a task, and during the initial phase of learning, students question their capabilities to use various skills and methods to complete the task. The student's perceptions will impact how they handle the assignment, either avoiding challenges if their beliefs are low, or persisting if they are more confident in their capabilities. Once the task is completed, the student can then look back on their actions, reflecting on how successfully they completed the task, and then this mastery experience can reinforce their beliefs when they take on the next piece of coursework.

Bandura (1993) reinforced that a person's perception and understanding of their self-efficacy influence both goal setting and analytic thinking. In learning, thoughts come before actions, and with thoughts, preparation, and consideration come strategic decisions involving choosing methods and planning how to carry out an action. This can include choosing important markers to signal progress as new information is put into practice and skills are used. These decisions are regulated through self-influence processes (Lock & Latham, 1990; Zimmerman, 1998).

As students begin to move from thought to action, if their motivation is focused on goals, it will be shaped by their perception and reaction to their performance. That is to say each time they arrive at the chosen marker, or checkpoint for progress, they reassess their self-efficacy in relation to their achievement so far. The next goal-marker can then be readjusted based on their reflections on progress and their revised self-efficacy views (see Bandura & Cervone, 1986). A hierarchical, structured series of proximal goals will increase self-efficacy for learning (Schunk, 1981) by allowing students to visibly measure their success in learning. This begins to create elements of an ideal learning situation where students consciously take responsibility for the processes of monitoring, reflecting, and eventually achieving their potential.

Self-efficacy manifests itself throughout the learning process when people effectively regulate and reflect upon their learning. To foster the formation and practical application of these beliefs within the teaching context, the details involving the who, the what, the how, and the process of their interaction must first be carefully considered and understood by the teacher before they can be effectively presented to the student. Having assignments with embedded markers or checks along the way allows longer-term motivation to be sustained and perpetuated. Realistic goals can be used to help teach students to learn for themselves by reducing the gap between what students know and the unknown to create situations where students are both likely and capable of success (Bandura, 1993). A person's perseverance and persistence will vary depending on self-efficacy beliefs (Bandura & Jordan, 1991; Greene & Miller, 1996), and this in turn will impact achievements. With a series of smaller goals and attainments, students will be more likely to continue with sustained self-efficacy beliefs instead of being stunted by deficiencies if goals are too distant or tasks are perceived as too difficult.

▶ The need for specificity

Educators need to know how the information gained from studying self-efficacy can apply more widely to practical settings. Over the decades, research has shown a more complete picture of self-efficacy and its influences, and practical studies have continued to separate these beliefs from the whole self-view. The specific nature of the beliefs, and exactly how they related to the given tasks, was questioned. Could the beliefs made in one setting transfer over to a wider setting or were they uniquely representative of only that one task?

Answers to these questions came partly as the concept of self-efficacy was refined. People began to understand there was a need to be really quite specific in understanding both the task and the context of the beliefs, and more attention was devoted to how people's self-efficacy beliefs were quantified (Bong, 2006). Advice was published on the way to measure self-efficacy beliefs, on construction of questionnaire, to test whether the questionnaires were valid or measuring the construct accurately, and throughout this the task-specific nature of self-efficacy was stressed (Bandura, 2006). The questions used in researching a person's level of self-efficacy need to correspond directly to a specific task in order to ensure that it is self-efficacy that is being measured and not a more broad personal concept. It is very difficult to discuss such a specific belief across all instances. Even within a subject area, there may be many different self-efficacy beliefs, for each of countless different tasks. Educational research suggests that self-efficacy should focus on specific tasks (Pajares, 1996b), and within academic settings there are often tasks that share a subset of similar skills.

The two types of experiences that all students encounter in education are learning and assessment. Schunk (1996a) was the first to separate types of self-efficacy beliefs within a subject, and he distinguished self-efficacy for learning from self-efficacy for performing. Schunk, Hanson, and Cox (1987), Zimmerman et al. (1992) and Schunk (1996a), and Ritchie & Williamon (2011) illustrated the need to distinguish self-efficacy for learning and per-forming in academic settings, and to maintain links to tasks. Specificity can help to detail relationships between the positive qualities, attributes, and influences, and avoids confusing students' perceptions of their general com-petences for self-efficacy beliefs.

Self-efficacy for learning

Making judgements about self-efficacy for learning requires the student to consider their capabilities for acquiring new skills and engaging with learning processes. This includes beliefs about understanding and applying learning methods, whereas self-efficacy for performing involves beliefs about execut-ing a task successfully by using skills that have already been learned (Schunk, 1996a). Self-efficacy for learning needs to be assessed before having specific instruction in new skills and processes (Schunk & Hanson, 1985; Schunk, 1996a). Being aware of student beliefs puts teachers in a better position to orient their teaching to best help and guide student progress.

In learning contexts, self-efficacy has been linked reciprocally to both motivation and self-regulation (Schunk, 1989; Zimmerman, 1989) and has predicted people's activity choices. It relates to persistence, especially when the task is sufficiently difficult that some students will quit before they com-plete it. In essay writing sometimes students begin researching well, and sometimes their enthusiasm and drive is not sustained; those with higher self-efficacy for learning beliefs will keep at the task despite the difficulties.

Students begin learning with their own levels of background knowledge and experience. As they progress, self-efficacy beliefs are influenced by inter-nal processes such as choices involving goal setting and information process-ing, as well as through external factors such as feedback or rewards. Schunk (1996b) explained that successful learning impacts student self-efficacy beliefs differently, depending on individual perceptions. For example, if students do not consider themselves to have made much progress, but believe they can still accomplish the task, self-efficacy will not be reduced even though pro-gress is slow.

Schunk (1996a) suggested that the methods used in Bandura's initial investigations within a psychotherapy context (1977) mostly assessed self-efficacy for performance and needed to be altered for academic settings. To assess self-efficacy for learning, Schunk (1996a) presented students with a sample problem for a short time so they could view the type of problem, but not have enough time to actually solve it, and then asked students to make a judgement on their capability to solve something similar (Schunk, 1981; Schunk & Rice, 1993). By asking students if they could solve a similar problem, the focus was on the specific skill base that was required for that context. Self-efficacy for learning sustains student motivation and leads to effective use of self-regulatory strategies (Zimmerman, 1989; Zimmerman & Martinez-Pons, 1990; Zimmerman et al., 1992). This correspondence of self-efficacy with specific skills and tasks was also studied in mathematics (Konstantopolous, 1996) and English (Shell et al., 1989; Schunk & Rice, 1993).

Students' perceptions of their self-efficacy for learning are influenced by experience (mastery), and require them to look forward to anticipate engagement with learning. To make an informed decision, students need to understand the requisite skills and processes for learning. A misrepresentation of self-efficacy can occur if students do not consider themselves challenged by tasks, and rightly or wrongly consider their assignments to be 'easy'. This can happen with a very large class size, if students are not fully engaged with the content, or have not kept up with the work, and it is possible for students to misjudge self-efficacy for learning due to overconfidence. Both the accuracy of perceptions and the way self-efficacy is assessed are important, whether this is through personal reflection or formal research. When student perceptions of self-efficacy are true, the predictive value of self-efficacy remains valid.

Self-efficacy for performing

With assessment, and any form of presentation or display of knowledge or skill, all students are performers. Self-efficacy for performing is about carrying out a task by implementing a set of already learned and rehearsed skills that remain constant during the performed task. This is different to self-efficacy for learning, where the skills are constantly changing and being developed. Familiarity with a task will impact the way someone judges his or her self-efficacy for performing. If people are familiar with the type of situation being assessed, they are more likely to have the knowledge and experience that enables them to make a judgement of their capabilities to perform the required task. However, with an unfamiliar task, students would be unable to pinpoint the skill set required, and a specific judgement might not be possible. If the situation is completely new, people might guess how they think the task is carried out, and could make a false or inaccurate assessment of self-efficacy. In this situation, it might be necessary therefore to generalise about how the task is performed, or to use a simulated or imagined example so that students can make self-efficacy for performing judgements.

The perception of these beliefs is strongest when assessed as near as possible to the moment of carrying out the task. This gives the closest and most true relationship of the student's belief in their capabilities to the actual action of the task. This works well for research studies that use questionnaires with statistical reports of correlations and causal links that are important to quantify and validate influential factors. In a practical teaching context there is no way that a teacher could regularly stop sessions, pass out questionnaires, and ask students to complete them before taking an exam or carrying out a task. Not only would this break the flow of any session, be stressful for the students, and quickly become artificial, the process would be of little or no use to anyone without a detailed analysis and follow-up of the results. This does not mean that self-efficacy beliefs themselves are inconsequential or that students should not be made aware of them. Students do not need to know complex statistical relevance of their self-efficacy beliefs, but it is useful to know that they actually achieved a higher result in an exam because of strong self-efficacy beliefs. Everyday materials and activities can help teachers shape students' practical understanding of how self-efficacy for performing beliefs can influence and impact achievement within a subject area.

▶ **In the classroom**

Fostering secure self-efficacy beliefs needs time, dedication, and detailed forethought. Consider, as an example, a child who learns music. As a teenager, they can perform with complete confidence and control because every experience with the instrument, since they started learning at the age of 3 or 5, was designed to put small building blocks in place to foster security and reinforce self-efficacy beliefs. Children raised in a musical family will often undertake hours of practice to gain the requisite skills on their instrument. Verbal guidance and encouragement comes from teachers during formal weekly music lessons and from parents in daily practice sessions. They will have opportunities to see the other students perform, and perhaps even to see family members perform in a professional setting. Finally, the student will take part in both informal and formal performances on a regular basis. All of the four main influences of self-efficacy are present and regularly reinforced. Beliefs are not built on one-off experiences, otherwise, the first time a musical performer made an unexpected slip they would quit forever.

The difference between a young violinist and a student in a lecture is that the violinist is viewed as a young performer from the outset, from first playing

'Twinkle Twinkle', whereas the student sitting in the third row back might only be thought of as a student who is in the class for the semester, and not as a biologist, an historian, or as a preacher. Yes, they have a long way to go before becoming professionals, and students need to learn, but when building a network of beliefs the teacher needs to keep that end goal in sight.

The influences that build self-efficacy beliefs are in themselves simple, and to be effective, experience with them needs to be frequent, merited, and reinforced. This can be a challenge in a teaching setting when time and contact with students is limited. Students also spend a disproportionate amount of time learning as compared to performing: a student may spend several hours per week over a period of months learning and then be assessed in a single one to three hour time slot. This is not an unrealistic reflection on the way pivotal decisions happen in professional contexts; job interviews are seldom based on a candidate's capacity for learning, but instead measure performance.

In educational settings students are taught measurable content, but also need to be taught the engagement and how to learn. To prepare for success in a profession they also need to have the grounding, experience, and belief in their capabilities to perform. Some students who either overestimate their capabilities (see Pajares, 1996b) or who suffer from low self-efficacy (Pajares & Miller, 1994) will benefit from understanding the accuracy of their self-perceptions.

Teaching self-efficacy for learning

Practical demonstrations that take students through each of the influences of self-efficacy for learning can be woven into any teaching setting. When sessions begin by setting students at ease, the students will be open to learning and not create unnecessary physiological barriers or doubts about their capabilities. The overview of a session, whether a list of expectations or learning outcomes, can be framed either in a way that is impersonal and dry, perhaps in a prepublished outline of the session, or on a PowerPoint presentation. The student might see that the session will include:

▶ presenting key points
▶ defining and contextualising them
▶ understanding how to use them

With very subtle changes the teacher could personally invite the student to engage by saying:

> Throughout this session you will acquire knowledge of the key points, their definition and context, and at the end of the session you will understand how to use them.

Directing the content of the bullet points towards the student is a small but essential positive reinforcement. Often teachers assume that students both know what to do in learning and understand that there is a basic expectation that they will succeed as long as they apply themselves with the tasks. How often do teachers actually tell students that they believe they will succeed? This affirmation is important as a beginning point. After the learning process begins, however, the teacher's verbal encouragement will be overridden by what the student does. If the students continue to engage, then further supportive comments will reinforce and sustain both the student's beliefs and the processes of learning.

Engaging the students actively in learning processes will enable them to notice the influential moments as they happen. Even in a large lecture setting where students are sitting and there is little opportunity for the teacher to alter this arrangement, students can be engaged in reflection and constantly monitoring the use and development of their skills in comparison to a model. The teacher could model, demonstrating engagement with a concept, by perhaps working out a mathematical theorem on the board. Through a guided commentary the teacher does not only physically write out the content, but also points out the processes, skills, and cognitive mechanisms that are involved in working out the solution. This shows students a model of someone successfully developing his or her learning and gives the students something they can compare directly to their own skills development.

Following on from this in-class modelling and demonstration, students could then be asked to undertake a homework task that reinforces the new concepts. This has the potential to be either a positive or negative experience. If the task is too difficult and students cannot determine and choose appropriate strategies, or if they do not have the understanding of how to proceed with the task, then failure is likely. Assignments do not need to be easy; however, the students need to either have a budding awareness of the necessary skills and methods or understand how to source the skills they need. Then, with all the learning tools they need, they can undertake the task. Still, if students do not have a high self-efficacy for learning, there will be a reluctance to approach a task that is not obvious, as it might lead to failure (Bensimon, 2007). Those with high self-efficacy for learning will persist and be resilient despite having to invest time and effort to arrive at a successful solution (Zimmerman, 2000).

Self-efficacy for learning can be developed through methods that encourage the student to observe their processes. When students reflect on aspects of their learning throughout different phases of their coursework, this will act as reinforcement for their self-efficacy beliefs and for their learning. Noting changes like an increased capacity for note taking and use of learning methods as part of a student's ongoing practice of reflection does not mean that the teacher's reinforcement or feedback is redundant. Sometimes students can know intellectually that they have engaged with processes, but are unable to accept this as a mastery experience that they have achieved and own. Even though a great deal of students' time is spent developing learning and building a skill base, the achievement of gaining a skill through learning is a task too. Teachers can iterate goals to students in a way that helps them to break down the ongoing process of learning and acknowledge that efficient use of time and capabilities is an achievement just like any other task.

Teaching self-efficacy for performing

Students are very aware of assessments in all their different forms: exams, essays, presentations, practical work, and each assessment will come with a set of requirements and criteria used to determine the mark for the submission. Sometimes students choose their classes based on the assessments, and thoughts or anxiety surrounding that final task can hang over the whole course. With self-efficacy for performing, teachers need to ask themselves if the students are being prepared to do those final tasks. It is completely possible that a student has very good comprehension of the material and can articulate this well in writing, but has very little experience in giving a talk with live demonstrations. The skill of delivering information in this way, of 'performing' that task, may not have entered into the taught content of the course. Imagine 'The history of the USSR and its successors' as a lecture course taught to a hall of 350 students, and at the end of the course students experienced something completely different and sat for a two-hour exam.

Contact time with students is limited, and in a lecture setting it is not commonly found that lecture time is devoted to teaching exam skills. This is just one example of a case where students are taught content but the mode of assessment is actually removed from that content, and it illustrates a need to consider the task and how it is approached. Methods that work to build learning skills cannot be directly translated in performing contexts. In preparation for performing, people need a repeated experience that allows them to use their skills as they execute the task. They need experience with several different tasks that all use the same skills, thus reinforcing the act of consistently performing that learned set of skills. A challenge for the teacher is not necessarily to think of the tasks, but how to integrate them in a meaningful way into the course. Students learn to perform, and this too needs time. Teachers cannot expect their students to simply have five runs through a task the day before and that this will ensure a polished performance. Students still need guidance and feedback on their engagement with tasks, whether these are accomplishments or failures.

**Box 2.1 Helping students become active participants
in feedback**

A teacher could require students to write 1000 words every week in preparation for a final essay of 3500 words. This would, on one hand, be
excellent experience for the students, but it is highly impractical for the
teacher as nobody can devote the time or energy to that level of extra
grading on top of the preparation that goes with delivering sessions. It
could, however, be that students are required to progressively write different amounts during the course. It might be that in the first week they
write 200 words and this is not graded by anyone. In the second week,
they write another 200 words, but this time there are criteria and each
student need to specifically decide how they were able to meet the criteria
and what they would need to do to improve. Next, a 500-word piece of
writing is produced, anonymised, and collected, or better yet produced
electronically, and the same process of comparison against criteria happens not by the author, but by peers. Each student is then responsible for
marking the work of two other students, being careful to attend to the
criteria and provide constructive and critical comments.

Essay writing is perhaps the easiest to integrate as an assignment that has
the scope for making students active participants in the reflection process.

This does rely on student engagement to be a successful activity. It gives
a range of experience to the students and prepares them to complete the
main assessed task for that class. They experience their final task from both
a student and assessor's point of view. The accumulation of written tasks,
experiences with the grading process, and critical commentary and discussion all provide opportunities for reflection. Throughout the process students
gain both a mastery and vicarious experience with the task, and they receive
feedback (verbal persuasion).

In addition to the peer marking exercise, students can be required to
submit a formal formative assessment that is intended to act as a mock
version of the final. This can either be a full-length submission or simply
a smaller version that recreates or draws upon elements of the final task.
Teacher feedback from this will act as guidance and reinforcement of the
progress the student has made in performing that task. This exercise of
writing and assessing is designed to prepare students for the conditions and

processes involved in the final task, but it can be written into the course as a required, supplemental activity, allowing it to be housed outside the taught teaching time.

Not all final assessment tasks are removed from the content of a course. Many practical subject areas include performing as a regular feature of the taught content. In sport, music, or dance, students learn practical skills that naturally build towards performance. Although there is a great deal of physical activity in these subject areas, there are instances when creating a smaller or simplified version of the final task does not use the same skills as completing the actual assessment. For example, by playing only part of a concerto or walking a 1000-metre sprint is inherently different to performing those tasks. Sometimes there is an aspect, like endurance or speed, that is integral to the task, and taking this out greatly reduces the value of the modified version in developing the student's self-efficacy for performing. It is essential that the tasks compare. The teacher needs, therefore, to consider the full nature of what performing requires and how students can gain meaningful mastery experiences that will strengthen their beliefs, leaving them prepared for the assessed performance.

3 Modes of communication and their influence on self-efficacy

This chapter examines interaction, communication, and feedback between teachers and their students within the context of learning and teaching. Various methods of engagement are described and contextualised in different practical teaching situations. Specific examples of everyday speech and movement are considered to demonstrate how a shift in awareness and applying simple, small changes can improve the effectiveness of communication and have a positive influence on self-efficacy beliefs.

The subtleties of communication allow students to be drawn into learning. Each student comes to learning with different circumstances, a unique knowledge base, their individual perceptions, and their own developing awareness and opinions. By combining various modes of communication, a teacher can communicate with their students to enable better understanding and practical application of the concepts presented. The goal in teaching in this way is that eventually the students will find their own vision; harnessing capabilities to digest, refine, and amalgamate what is learned into an emerging professional practice. Teaching is a process that involves far more than passing on information or answers. When teachers become sensitive to the nuance of communication's influence on learning, and to a student's individuality, then the process of using various means of communication to enhance self-efficacy beliefs becomes an intuitive and organic part of learning and teaching.

Everyday teachers speak and enhance learning through facial expression and physical gesture. Intentions are conveyed through half-sounds, and perhaps through laughter or even in silence. In effective teaching, communication can be developed as a two-way form of engagement and a mechanism to allow deeper levels of learning and exchange to be fostered between teachers and students. Opportunities for reflection can be created when students are invited to actively interact and own their learning processes.

This chapter is not intended to be a complete guide or prescriptive method for teaching, but to introduce and draw attention to ways of considering ordinary elements that may already exist within teaching. There are practices that may routinely and naturally occur in some disciplines that can be cultivated across subjects, bringing these to new teaching environments as tools to connect with and support students, and encourage them to generate ideas and facilitate their achievement. These will enhance the students' self-efficacy beliefs, moving away from a setting where students are taught 'at', and prepare them for an active role in their future.

Verbal persuasion is one of the four main influences on self-efficacy beliefs (Bandura, 1986), but it is less influential than having accomplished the task. For a student who is still learning the subject, the advice of others, and especially that coming from someone respected and knowledgeable, such as the teacher, is a very strong formative influence because students do not yet have a history of their own experiences to either positively or negatively supersede the teacher's advice. Whereas when an established professional receives comments from another teacher, these words may not have a great impact on their self-efficacy beliefs because the professional already has an established record of successful accomplishments that override the views of a single person. If, however, a very prominent researcher is the one who makes the remarks, this may be valued in a different way. Any comments are considered within the context of all of the existing influences on that person's self-efficacy. When weighed against the other influences, advice or remarks coming from a respected person who has a far greater mastery of the subject may have more impact on the professional's perceived self-efficacy. Teachers are in a privileged position and there is a great deal of advice communicated both directly and indirectly to students, who often have little mastery or practical experience of their subject matter. The teacher might be the first person to exert an influence on their student's self-efficacy beliefs, and the importance of the teacher's communications cannot be underestimated.

Feedback is not limited to the comments that appear on an exam paper; teachers are always in the spotlight of student awareness, and every aspect of communication can be used to assist, direct, and encourage the students toward developing a secure sense of their learning within a subject area. There are vast differences between the interactions that happen within learning and the experience of assessment, where there is a sense of finality and of performance. Depending on where the student is on their learning journey, this will influence how and why the teacher chooses to focus and pitch communication in a certain way. There will be times when the student's attention needs to be drawn to specific processes and skills, and other times when the refinement and delivery of the finished work is key. Methods of communicating that enable a focus on the students and their learning are relevant and are at the core of meaningful learning.

▶ Instruction, interaction, and feedback

Within different teaching settings, the perception and reception of feedback and interaction will be different, and the challenges of adapting to engage one, ten, or one hundred students will be explored. Even when the same type of room, subject, and student numbers are replicated, there are individual differences between teachers and with each new cohort of students. Teaching methods that allow for more creativity and expression with communication can be squeezed out of the lecture hall because of imposed pressures to focus on curriculum, assessment, or time constraints, or simply because of a growing class size. In smaller group settings, like seminars, tutorials, or one-to-one teaching, there is an element of uniqueness, and this creates a potentially private-feeling setting for both learning and the development of teaching methods (Hallam, 1998). There are many successful teachers in higher education that use their circumstances and environments to develop excellent efficacious students.

▶ In person

Live communication is experiential, spontaneous, and unfolding. It is different from reading a text, when there is the luxury of scanning ahead or reading back over certain paragraphs, or from observing a physical object where one can stand back and look at the work as a whole, taking in all of the component parts at once. There are aspects where interaction between people resembles performance, and can be compared to a dance or piece of live music. When a student stands up and presents, a machinist executes a delicate manoeuvre, or a businessman or clinician speaks with a client, each is performing, and these acts unfold in real time. The guidance and responses that teachers communicate to students both in and out of lessons impacts the student's self-efficacy for the tasks they carry out in class and later in the professional context.

Any time the teacher and student interact in person, there is an element of reciprocal influence. In a teaching setting when the teacher is a critical listener to a student who is performing, sometimes there are stunningly polished moments and seconds later there may be blemishes, with inconsistency or discontinuity in the delivery processes of the task. The teacher can use various methods to suggest improvements, but even the act of interjecting a few words causes a disturbance in the flow of the delivery. When commenting to highlight, add, or alter a technical detail, there is always a gap between the comment and its integration within the student's delivery when the student considers and decides how to proceed. A teaching situation cannot be suspended, maintaining the energy, beliefs, and momentum; all freezes in time while an exchange of feedback unfolds through verbal or physical interactions, and then somehow resumes and expects the student to carry on unchanged. Interaction has an impact on the seen and unseen aspects of the people involved; there is a relationship between the people, their actions, and the environment (Bandura, 1986, 1997).

Spoken word

The words we choose, and how and when we say them, can have a profound impact on our students. All that we say is, in effect, verbal feedback, whether part of a casual conversation or a specifically crafted response. It can include positive or negative criticism, instruction or guidance, suggestions, or simply acknowledgement of a situation. This applies to general comprehension, but also to developing students' self-efficacy beliefs. These beliefs do not have the simplicity of a multiple-choice paper with clear answers or influences that let people progress in a linear fashion. Simple diagnostic, direct communication may work, but it cannot be assumed as the most effective with every student. With the spoken word it is useful to consider each situation holistically and individually. What does the student know? Where are they coming from? What is the current situation? Are there any external factors involved? All of these can influence decisions about choosing words that will effectively and efficiently enable that student to see a situation clearly. This often involves *not* giving a direct answer, but drawing attention to the surroundings. The directness and immediacy of words is not always the best way. Providing a model or a comparison can be more productive than stating the direct facts (Huxham, 2007). Sometimes a student cannot extrapolate the meaning of comments (Zhao, 2010), and even if they do understand intellectually, they may not be able to internalise the information to use in their future practice.

This principle has a practical demonstration in astronomy. When star gazers want to see a distant faint star in the night sky, they do not look *at* the star, but they look at the darkness to the side of the star, using a technique called *averted* vision that was first introduced by Aristotle (Schaefer, 1993), and in time the eye will adjust to the darkness, and then the light that was previously too faint can be taken in. Likewise, each teaching situation is distinct, with sensitivities around how immediately one can state or communicate facts so that students can meaningfully comprehend and reflect on them.

Before considering specific situations, there are initial principles that will help to shape the ways we use language and the impact language can have on the students. Teachers can consciously choose words, taking into account any implied or associative meanings. For example, if words are to foster self-efficacy, then it makes sense to use the language of self-efficacy (see Bong, 2006). With these beliefs the focus is on *can* and being *capable*. When introducing topics, language that positively reinforces this will create a mindset that encourages receptivity and growth.

Working to present positives, as opposed to negatives, can have a strong impact on students. If instructed, 'don't turn on the flame before the experiment is prepared', then mentally students first imagine carrying out the action of turning on the flame before they can undo this to imagine not doing it. How can one conceive of *not doing* something? This principle was demonstrated by Wegner, Schneider, Carter and White (1987) when they told their test subjects they could think of anything they wanted except for a white bear. Inevitably people's minds were flooded with thoughts of white bears. Besides not wanting to reinforce negativity, communicating in this way is a deterrent to efficient learning, as a separate step is added to the understanding process. Throughout daily interactions, teachers can assess how often negatives present themselves in speech, and with a moment's thought intervening before action, these can be turned into positives. This does imply that all comments must be positively biased. Simply reframing a directive like, *'Don't turn on the flame'* to state, *'Keep the flame off'* can have a strong impact on student perception. The student can envisage one action and there are no hidden implications here. It is a clear instruction, whereas *don't* can imply that actually the teacher holds an unseen belief that the student might indeed do the wrong thing first. If the student believes that the teacher has doubts about their capabilities, this can inform and reinforce whatever self-efficacy beliefs that student already has in the learning context.

Another simple verbal change is to avoid asking students to *try* to do things. The idea that there is no 'try' relates very well to teaching situations and to developing self-efficacy beliefs, as trying implies a permanent state of non-action, non-success, and non-progress. It implies working hard, but it is not a committal, clear word, and perhaps it is not the instructor's intention for students to visualise using a great deal of effort in their work. What does it look like when someone tries to do something? It is not an image of accomplishment. Instead, use words that specify the stages of carrying out a task. For example, students do not *try* to write the essay, but students *do* brainstorm, plan, outline, research, draft, read, edit, and type the essay. By adding specificity to words, teachers ensure that students are directed clearly and avoid any unnecessarily implied or assumed negativity that comes with the non-achievement of *try*.

Physical gesture

When preparing students to be in a leadership or teaching role, an important yet difficult lesson for them to learn is that a teacher is always being watched and the audience is keenly aware of all aspects of what the teacher does. One student-presenter who had not fully considered the visibility of physicality and its impact on the audience gave an assessed talk, and during a video clip when the light dimmed, the student found a yo-yo in a jacket pocket. Forgetting that the audience was still watching, the student gave that yo-yo a spin. This naïve and unplanned action had an unintended negative impact on the audience. People wondered if the student presenting had an appropriate level of respect for the situation, if this was an unwarranted display of overconfidence, or if it was just plain intended to offend. In fact, it was completely unplanned and the student was unaware of having done anything and believed that the lights being turned down provided invisibility. There could have been a thousand things in the minds of the onlookers, but the point is that any unplanned or unconsidered habit – the scratch of the head, a hand held out-stretched, leaning firmly on a table – these can all be seen and have an impact on the listener.

Teachers can use gestures positively to support, highlight, and direct the attention of the student, and to reinforce the message and attitude we want to convey. Physical motions and non-verbal communication can be responsible for up to 65 per cent of the meaning in a relationship (Guerrero & Floyd, 2006). During a student's time in a degree programme, there will often be several years over which the relationship with a teacher develops, and both the student and the teacher will have a fairly intimate understanding of the mannerisms and the gestural signals that each other uses (Babad, 2009). The directness of words is useful, but sometimes it is difficult to communicate in fixed words about abstract concepts or expression. When students self-directed much of their learning at higher levels of learning, a gesture can be used in place of a direct verbal reply to leave enough space for the student to interpolate a meaning and make it their own. This involves planning, process, and a willingness of the teacher to let go and share control of the situation with the student.

In terms of gestures, body language and physical coding are well documented and defined within business and psychology literature (see Morris, 1994). The roots of physical gestures and their associated meanings extend throughout human interaction, and even into behaviour exhibited by primates (Knapp & Hall, 2005). Zhukov (2012) studied the verbal and non-verbal behaviours between students and teachers in a higher education context, coded non-verbal behaviours, and validated them in order to analyse and describe people's actions as observed in private instrumental lessons.

The specific behaviours found in the context of any private tuition setting will be specific to that learner and teacher, in that session on that day, but Zhukov's results showed that the gestural categories were indeed appropriate beyond music and across situations; the use of physical actions transcended the confines of a specific discipline. If gestures do generalise, this allows for teachers to learn from colleagues in diverse disciplines, and a common gestural approach and vocabulary for communicating in learning and teaching can be used in a range of settings. Gesture is not something to be confined to stage performers. Any time teachers are seen, whatever choices are made, to actively do or not to do: this is our gesture.

In a teaching situation, all of the factors, including the people, the place, and the people's thoughts and actions are interwoven to influence the efficacy of communication. Teachers can examine each aspect of the teaching situation and how they interact within it, separating the different components or aspects of the situation that are changeable from those that are fixed. This process of analysis can help teachers to develop an acute awareness of their existing practice, and teachers can reflect on how gestures, reactions, and movements are used in daily situations. Then teachers can consider the impact of their gestural vocabulary on students' perceptions and beliefs, and learning can be considered and refined.

A gestural vocabulary does not have to be complicated or choreographed. Subtle changes can include redirecting our physical positioning within the room. For example, how does student perception change if a teacher is fixed behind a lectern, standing off to the side, or even moving around? Is the teacher sitting or standing while speaking? There are elements of interaction and communication, even through eye contact, that reinforce the relevance and importance of the subject matter, and can show a student how something matters or that the subject relates to them. This is important, because when a teaching relationship is established, the communication during the learning and teaching process gives signals to the students. However, if the teacher refrains from any interaction, and acts as a live audio book, reading page by page, head down or fixed, and standing still, then there is no reason students should believe that there is any interest in them individually, and the positive impact of any feedback received on beliefs will be minimal if there is any impact at all.

Physical action can be effective either when speaking or listening. To enhance a teacher's communication to students, a gesture can emphasise or show the meaning of the words used, illustrating connections or demonstrating certain aspects of what is being said. When listening, there are times when speaking would be a disruption and actually be detrimental to the situation. When words are not preferable but the student needs guidance, and without committing to the definite meaning of words, a teacher can direct the attention where it is needed by using a gesture. Imagine the student understands the basics of a topic and is at the beginning of deeper comprehension. In this situation, a stop in the student's thought process can be avoided if in fact the teacher does not speak, but uses gesture. A nod, hand movement, or facial expression can encourage and affirm students during the course of a conversation, presentation, or even when observing or facilitating group work.

Listening

> Talking is not necessarily the only form of participation and silence does not necessarily mean being mentally disengaged. (Marlina, 2009, p.9)

Using the concept of the astronomer's sideways glance referred to above (in p.46), and allowing students to *see* for themselves, requires a willingness to allow time and freedom in interactions. Between saying something and a reply comes thought and reflection, and facilitating the processes of understanding is important. Whether on a large or small scale, the way in which a lecturer can effectively explore a topic, engage each student, and actively make any interchange personally relevant encourages both meaning and awareness on a deeper level. This can be through something students can relate to and see as relevant to their experience or something that is valuable as information or a tool to reach their goals. Through listening and choosing how to respond to student reactions the teacher can facilitate and guide this process.

Students' word choice, gesture, and work will all contribute to demonstrating their beliefs. The type of comments students make act as clues to their perceptions, progress, and outlook. Using strategic thinking or shying away from the tasks at hand are symptomatic of high and low self-efficacy, respectively (Bandura, 1993; Zimmerman, 2000). The self-efficacy beliefs may stem from a host of sources, but focusing student attention on the task and the skills involved can reorient their thinking. Careful listening and apprehending the meaning of student comments and the mechanisms they use to communicate invite the teacher's input. The teacher's reply should not be seen as a definitive answer, but as the catalyst for what students do next. This acts as an open door for the teacher to mould and guide student learning and outlook by steering and reframing their perception. When this is combined with positive experiences and a developing sense of self-efficacy, it can perpetuate a more positive, structured outlook toward learning.

In between speech and silence

A key to guiding and shaping meaningful interactive teaching relies on shifting the focus of teaching away from the teacher, not just by asking the student to speak, but by allowing the student to first think and reflect, and then to respond. If a student pauses before speaking, this does not imply passivity or vacancy, but it is the time when someone internally questions and processes the elements of the conversation (Schön, 1987). Tobin (1987) explains that as students learn about more complex situations and problems, there are higher levels of thinking required, and without time to think a student is disadvantaged.

This is relevant in conversational interaction as well as in larger lecture settings, which are still a main mode for delivery in higher education (Smith & Valentine, 2012; Weimer, 2013). A pause in a conversation is natural when waiting for a response, but in a lecture there will be fewer conversational moments. When addressing a large group, the pace of speaking slows (Atkinson, 2004); people need time to absorb the content, process, and make connections for themselves. Conversely, if a teacher adopts the position of presenting a monologue without consideration for the student's need to process, then the student is likely to get lost as the content becomes overwhelming.

Interestingly, in synchronous (real-time) online discussions students can control the time they need by waiting before typing a comment or reply. The person on the other end of the screen cannot physically 'read' them, so they wait to receive the next typed message. Students specifically appreciate the pause time that is integrated into an online environment because it allows time to reflect on new information before they reply (Meyer, 2003), whereas in a live situation there is not necessarily that time to process. In conversation, pauses generally extend no more than a second or two, with anything longer feeling awkward. In learning contexts, more time may be needed. When the lecturer is adopting more of a facilitator role, the times they do speak are very important. Making every word count by adjusting 'intonation, inflexion, phrasing, pacing, volume, loudness and timbre … Print does not allow a learner to identify and interpret audible nuances that personalise content because print cannot stimulate the auditory senses' (Power, 1990, p.45). Teaching can take a slightly different approach from a typical conversation to integrate that thinking time in a positive manner. This will facilitate learning and support students' beliefs in their capabilities to process the information. Physical signals such as not looking impatient or hurried, and will reinforce the neutrality of the pause, allowing the gaps to be a natural part of the learning discourse.

What is your natural speaking pace?

▶ Sent through the ether

There is a sense of permanency with any recorded commentary. Once words are recorded in print, audio, or video they can be reviewed and scrutinised, and the sender is no longer there to direct or guide that process of receiving the feedback. Disengagement severs that important continuum of learning and development that happens when communication is delivered live, in person. When communication is asynchronous, it becomes increasingly difficult to gage the reaction of students as they consider and reflect on what they have received. There is also the possibility that students may not read, listen to, or watch the feedback at all. It is essential then that students are motivated to engage with feedback and believe that the comments that teachers provide are meaningful to them and play an active role in supporting and shaping their practice and beliefs.

Typed or annotated files

Traditionally, students receive written comments on their graded assessments. Completing an assignment is a form of mastery experience, and when a student submits their assignment, self-efficacy beliefs will range from full confidence to being completely full of doubt. There are times when people do have unrealistic views of their capabilities and may have high self-efficacy beliefs yet still do poorly on an assignment (Pajares, 1997). Typed feedback is a form of verbal persuasion and acts as a check on the students' beliefs. The teacher's remarks can also influence students' self-efficacy for learning and can inform how they approach similar processes in the future.

Students do want comments that are specifically about their work and performance and that are individual to them (Pitts, 2005; Ferguson, 2011; Race, 2014), but even when these are provided, there is evidence that students do not necessarily read or know how to use the teacher's comments (Holmes & Papageorgiou, 2009). For example, in Weaver's (2006) study of 44 students in "Business, Art & Design", half of the students did not understand how they could engage with their feedback and many found teacher comments negative and unhelpful.

When providing written comments on a final piece of work, it is challenging to use that communication to effectively embed skills and further the learning, because sometimes the students do not see the teacher again. In this case, the official learning has ended, and students may be concerned with the grade on the paper, but not with attending to the advice given in comments. Students' self-efficacy can still be developed, but there is often little opportunity for dialogue following typed comments that accompany work.

With the physical element of communication removed, there is a greater importance on the words chosen and their usage to ensure the student's interpretation matches what is intended, as typed words can only stand at face value.

A teacher's response may be straightforward when the work is well pre-pared and demonstrates student capabilities, and perhaps comments may even follow a pro-forma. Feedback might align with specific assessment crite-ria, relate mainly to outcomes, and explain and support the grade awarded. Comments like 'the presentation was well timed' or 'the essay makes appro-priate use of technical language and draws upon primary sources' confirm the success level of the work, and will confirm the student's self-efficacy for performing, but do not particularly help to develop the student's self-efficacy for learning beliefs.

Clear writing that directs the student through the stages of learning can dissect what led to producing the assignment he or she did or explain how and what processes could be undertaken to alter the work. This can impact the student's learning and understanding, allowing growth and a strategic way forward. Even with a poor result, if there is a clear strategic approach, then the student will have more of a chance to take that path than if it had never been presented. Those with higher self-efficacy use more critical think-ing to find ways of achieving the end result. The comments of a teacher that clearly present these methods can develop beliefs of people with lower self-efficacy by guiding them through the processes that they need to achieve for themselves. Where annotation is an option, this gives more insight into the specifics, and represents more of a dialogue; however, any printed com-mentary that is one-sided will always pose challenges involving clarity for the teacher, and challenges of interpretation and application for the student

Recorded audio or video files

Several problems associated with typed comments can be avoided with audio feedback. Lunt and Curran (2010) found students ten times more likely to open and listen to an audio file than to collect written feedback. There is a personal element in audio files, where the student can hear the inflection, pace, and stresses of the voice, and thus there is less inherent ambiguity than with printed text. When a video file is an option, this encompasses physi-cality, even if only captured on a flat screen and 'there is a sense in which being "spoken to" is felt to be a more direct engagement with the student' Ribchester, France, and Wakefield (2008).

Recorded commentary is still not a replacement for direct interac-tion and the importance of the two-way discussions in learning and developing the student's sense of beliefs (see Chapter 4 p.73). There are still drawbacks of having a one-sided discussion via video. Although there is a sense of interaction, there is no possibility of a conversation or of shaping the content according to the way the student reacts, either with further explanation, a change in the pace of delivery, or by adding expression. These aspects are left to guesswork, based on what the teacher knows of the student. However, as face-to-face feedback sessions are not practical within the context of higher education (Ribchester et al., 2008), providing audio or video files can be a viable alternative to the traditional typed commentary.

...thinking about it

- ▶ What is your silent reading pace?
- ▶ How does this change if you speak the words you read?
- ▶ Does this change if you are speaking with someone?
- ▶ How does this change if you remove the visual and close your eyes while having a conversation?
- ▶ How is the process of understanding different?
- ▶ What do you miss visually and how is meaning maintained through inflection, pace, and pause time?

▶ Applications to teaching settings

Teachers can enhance students' self-efficacy in practical settings by highlighting specific processes that are related to the qualities associated with self-efficacy. As a student progresses through their learning, the teacher can be an external observer, using verbal and physical communication to guide and direct students' awareness to examples of their using creative thought processes to negotiate challenging situations, examples of resilience, and examples of accomplishment. This can serve as a model and catalyst for what will become self-sustained, self-regulated learning.

Individual settings

In higher education, tutorials are one of few opportunities for students and teachers to meet in a one-to-one context. Some institutions require students to attend regular tutorials, and others allow and encourage students to request meeting with the teacher for a tutorial. Across disciplines, tutorials can be more or less formal, but across the sector it is a setting where collaborative interaction takes place and the teacher is likely to be receptive to the specific student's queries or concerns (Benwell, 1999). The teacher's attention can be devoted to that student's work and development as opposed to in a larger lecture setting where the teacher may deliver a structured lecture.

When teachers and students meet for a tutorial, to guide or support coursework, talk is an important mode of communication. Words are so commonplace and yet can be counterproductive if not used thoughtfully and appropriately. Boore (1993) suggests that tutorials should include questioning, listening, responding, and explaining, where both the student and teacher are involved. It takes a craftsman to use words in a way that lead instead of tell, allowing exploration and discovery without either dictating orders or simply providing the answer.

Some disciplines, particularly within the arts, include aspects of regular individual contact that is more than a tutorial to supplement another lecture. In music, for example, the individual lesson is traditionally the main mode of instruction, where a core curriculum is delivered through interaction and feedback (see Gaunt, 2008). There is also a call for active reflection and participation from the student. A student may study with the same teacher for the duration of time in higher education and a true working relationship develops between the student and the teacher can develop. Individual tuition allows for some of the most flexible, experimental teaching.

A one-to-one setting can also create a setting where the student relies on the teacher, but formulating self-beliefs needs to be done by the student; these are personal beliefs and cannot be provided or dictated by a teacher. If students are constantly following someone else's directives, then the processes and achievements could be attributed to the teacher, not to them (Bong, 2006). Guiding students to experience and be aware of these processes allows them a perspective that they can own. Giving answers is far easier than facilitating someone's belief, but independence allows that students can and will be able to take learning forward, further building self-efficacy beliefs on their own.

Disciplines like art, drama, sport, or music have strong physical components that may not be present in the same way in other theoretical or text-based pursuits. Teachers who work in artistic or performance subject areas are often more free to use innovative and creative means to communicate in a student-centred manner that engages and challenges their students to simultaneously develop skills and establish their beliefs. Working outside of words frees teachers from the associations and assumptions of direct communication. It is not so unusual that someone teaching music may use gesture to illustrate the sound the student is aiming to create. This could be to convey a meaning in the absence of a specific vocabulary to describe the sound, and so the gesture is meant to express or be associated with the qualities of what is desired.

A poignant example of the clever use of various means of communication to facilitate the student coming to know, experience, and understand comes from the cello teacher William Bruce. In his one-to-one lessons, he will occasionally make a complete break from his teaching routine. He alters the student's awareness by using a single, simple gesture that effectively changes everything about lesson's interaction. When the student arrives for the lesson, Bruce puts his finger to his lips to indicate that there will be no verbal communication. Suddenly everything looks, sounds, and feels different. Both the teacher and the student are in a position where listening and awareness are at the forefront. It breaks any chance of the student relying on the habit of a routine where it may be possible to not engage but only go through the motions. Suddenly the student is required to listen, respond, and find new ways of questioning, and this activity uses all of the communication faculties of both student and teacher.

In many settings across the arts, humanities, and sciences, words come first and then the learning that internalises and reinforces the spoken instruction is developed as a separate, secondary act. There is a tendency to objectify and describe through words. Performance subjects are not immune to this, and talking, and specifically 'teacher talk', is a main feature observed in music lessons, at times even above the time spent playing music (Persson, 1993; Karlsson & Juslin, 2008).

Hans Jensen, Professor at the Bienen School of Music, Northwestern University, is another example of a music teacher who combines all of the possible methods of interacting with his students, integrating words, sounds, silence and gestures into a synthesis that allows him to communicate with students in an exchange that is effective and fluid. He ensures that interaction minimises the disruption to the musical performance process on both a large and small scale. Having to start and stop the physical action of playing an instrument every time a comment is made can interrupt, wasting time and energy, and breaking the continuity of student learning.

Jensen is clever in using familiarity as a tool to draw out his students' ideas instead of dictating to them. Then through discussion and exploration of these ideas in the lesson, students can solidify their own conceptions about their capabilities and expressive goals in music making. They are guided to become aware of, and reinforce, their self-efficacy beliefs. Jensen is keenly aware that each student, his or her individual instrument, and the content of the music studied, all represent different sides of a very multifaceted overall picture. His lessons illustrate how sensitivity and carefully considered actions and reactions can allow the dynamic of the one-to-one setting to become a malleable and creative vehicle to further student growth and learning.

Jensen explained the rationale behind his use of familiarity and references external to music:

> If the music is compared to Impressionism in art, there is a certain colour and texture in the painting and in sound, on a string instrument. Technically, you have a much faster and lighter bow speed and a finer vibrato, and the result is almost like the colours [in the painting]. A performer can really do that in sound. When people relate how those pictures look to how the sound sounds, they can apply it. This only works with the people who have a sense of painting and might even have experienced painting themselves. You can't tell someone who doesn't understand, 'Ok, now you are going to go to museums for three weeks to understand that'. (Jensen, 2013)

It is important that the external reference, or analogy, used by the teacher is relevant, understood, and meaningful to that student; no one reference will be suitable for all students. Jensen draws associative links for his students from their everyday experiences:

> I might say to a student, to evoke the sense of sound, 'What fruit do you like?' If she has a favourite fruit, then what would it sound like, and can she make it into sound? Then because it is their favourite they have a really strong attachment to that image and they can actually put that into a sound, but if you use the same image for everybody it will not work. If you always use chocolate as an image for sound, then the people that don't like chocolate, won't make a very good sound! (Jensen, 2013)

With any technique there can be verbal, technical explanations to provide a step-by-step analysis of how to do something, but this can quickly become a list and moves the teaching away from a student-centred approach. When the student can make connections using strategic thinking and experimentation, then the persistence and resilience they demonstrate, alongside teacher guidance and support, will build positive self-beliefs about how they can achieve and obtain results.

Seminars

Feedback in a small group, or seminar, setting can help students to understand their capabilities and what they have done, thus informing how they make their self-efficacy judgements. To support students and develop their sense of self-efficacy, it is important to align comments with the sources of self-efficacy: the task, the skills, and processes that go into carrying out that task. The words we choose and how feedback is given may vary dramatically from student to student and the dynamics of the situation.

In a practical situation where students are required to stand up and present in front of a few peers, they will have expectations based on the pattern of previous session. They will be familiar with the setting and as long as the student is prepared, the teacher may comment on various elements of the content and the presentation itself. Feedback in this setting, about the performance of the task, directly relates to aspects of what the student just experienced and will reinforce the student's self-efficacy beliefs.

What if the session is moved to another location? This change could make some students feel less confident. Even though this is an external factor, and not something the student can actively control (Williamon, 2004), he or she must still show resilience to maintain self-efficacy for performing in that situation. Imagine a scenario where the venue is changed due to a timetabling clash, and the new room has a different physical arrangement, different acoustic, and a different temperature. The student's prepared content remains the same, but as the presentation begins, the student feels insecure and has doubts, and communicates this by saying, *'It's not going well; I'm not sure what it is.'* Needless to say, the presentation does not go very well, and it is certainly not as the student had planned. The teacher could choose to provide feedback on the many technical errors that happened on this occasion, but this would not be the most meaningful or beneficial for the student. It is clear that the student experienced a lack of self-efficacy for performing at that moment, and pointing out the flaws would only confirm and reinforce these low self-beliefs (Pitts, 2005; Ferguson, 2011).

Self-efficacy is built on experiences, but the student's assessment of the problems in his or her presentation can be misattributed to factors that are beyond someone's control, such as: *I did badly because I was in a new space.* If the material is prepared, and the student was prepared for factors that might be out of his or her control (like the person who unwraps a sweet in the front row of a concert) then there is no reason this should be the reason for the problems. Still, the student may *perceive* the venue to be the cause of the problems, and not take responsibility for his or her actions. Considering and understanding the student view and receptiveness to learning and to the situation, to what influenced the student's confidence and self-efficacy, will enable the teacher to make an informed choice about how to give feedback in the most constructive way. Still, if something unforeseen shakes the confidence of a student, it does not mean that the unpolished presentation and the ensuing errors can be simply ignored. After that negative experience, the student needs to understand *why* his or her self-efficacy beliefs were affected and how to move forward. Identifying and discussing the other factors will enable the student to be aware of the factors and how he or she contributes to the situation: what can be controlled and prepared for and what is a fixed external factor within the situation. This can help the student to correctly attribute the causes of what went wrong and see how to correct this next time in order to solidify self-efficacy beliefs before he or she encounters the task again.

Giving feedback about the circumstances distances the student from his or her actions and helps to open a discussion about the situation and how it impacted his or her perceptions. Explaining how a different audience or room can challenge views about capabilities, and how in preparing for any delivery it is important to remind one's self about the core skills that are being used, to ensure that these can be delivered independently of the changeable, external factors. This can help the student to make clear judgements and think strategically when planning the performance. Also, being able to attribute the difficulty to a fixed, external factor means that it was not necessarily a personal deficiency, and this will lessen the negative impact of that experience on overall self-efficacy for performing beliefs.

In the opposite situation, where a student is unphased by a change of venue and remains confident, secure, and even seems to thrive on the newness of the situation, verbal feedback can be used to reinforce the strong sense of self-efficacy. The teacher can point out the accomplishment, and the steps the student took to create a successful presentation, like the successful navigation of the new surroundings and not letting these interfere with the prepared content. Specifics of how the presentation was effective and demonstrated that student's preparation can be raised in comments. *'You were secure in your delivery and this meant that you were able to communicate your ideas effectively to the audience.' 'You adapted to the dynamic of this space and altered your voice appropriately considering the arrangement of the audience.'* Critical comments can still be made in a positive way as well, *'When unexpected things happened, you did not give this away through body language or in your spoken delivery, but you allowed the presentation to flow as if it was planned to be that way.'*

Large lectures

The large lecture setting affords all the advantages of live communication, but it does come with its own challenges. Once the group size has increased beyond about a dozen, then members of the audience can become anonymous (Atkinson, 2004). When this happens, the impact on a student's self-efficacy of any learning experiences presented in the lecture can be greatly reduced, as there is the chance that the lecture can be perceived as irrelevant or simply as a fact-gathering session. For students to take something positive from the lecture *they* need to make the connections. The teacher can still facilitate this, but it is more difficult to react and adapt to each individual in this setting.

The teacher can help students to stay on track and take the most from the lecture by iterating the processes. In a simple presentation, there could be a demonstration in the front of a lecture theatre where onlookers watch passively. Consider a traditional lecture where the lecturer begins presenting, fully aware that the audience is too large to individually acknowledge, continues by unfolding the technical or factual content, and ends. Large student numbers in a lecture hall occur across disciplines: physics, history, sport, education, English – the situation is common. Students take notes while the teacher speaks, writes notes on a board, or follow a PowerPoint presentation that might appear on an intranet site for students to access after the session. The main purpose of the classic lecture session is to deliver the information.

In this situation, without interaction or a reason to engage, the students are almost given the invitation to mentally wander off. If there is no benefit to being in the live situation, then perhaps reading a book is just as good? Staying mentally focused in a lecture like this requires effort, motivation, and usually a good deal of groundwork on the part of the student. Texts must be read and the students need to be poised for the learning. Even with preparation, students may not be able to instantly digest or even follow the material, and if students cannot understand the material, then how is that going to affect their self-efficacy for learning or for completing assessment tasks? This poses real challenges for the teacher presenting.

Students with a strong sense of self-efficacy may find the situation challenging, but they will find ways to access the content and learn. They will use other sources, searching for texts to facilitate their understanding, accessing additional support through tutorials or seminars, and will exhaust all avenues for learning before they actually give up. Whereas for those who already have low self-efficacy, being in a lecture where the culture is to sit and not interrupt can make them feel alone in a crowd of listeners. These students can perceive the content to be overwhelming and feel a genuine lack of support. These feelings will confirm their own perceived limitations. Without interaction with the students to gain feedback and awareness, the teacher may not realise the situation. Despite a clear presentation of information, students can still be left with so much work before they are in a position to approach the tasks and achieve.

There are some aspects of the large lecture that cannot be turned into a one-to-one discussion, and the teacher will never individually meet the needs of every student in that setting. Even without the use of real-time technological interaction, a traditional lecture presentation can be tailored so that students do feel engaged and a part of what is happening. Once there is an active relationship between the student, the teacher, and the content, a meaning can be established. With personal investment in the session, students will begin to make decisions about their capabilities to take on board the content and perform the tasks.

Teachers can decide to take action and make the most of their capabilities as facilitators. How can a teacher plan for this? It is not practical to invite conversations throughout a lecture, as this can easily take over the session and prevent the content from being covered. Silent and shaped participation can be effective for the student. Students do not need everything explained to them, but they do need to actively engage with some of the process being demonstrated. If the teacher builds some of the process into the information, then it can be as if the conversation is acted out with one person taking both sides. The students still have to do the work to create meaning for themselves, but this way the path to understanding becomes far clearer.

Practically, a presenter who is aware will use inflection and gesture to guide the student's attention to elements within the content while speaking, but also the presenter can explain in a way that vicariously walks the student through the experience. In an applied problem-solving situation, instead of directly announcing the solution, the thinking behind the processes or choices can also be discussed. This allows students to have examples of how to use metacognition and strategic thinking (Schunk & Usher, 2013), and they can then apply the same methods to similar situations when studying on their own.

Monitoring student understanding can be incorporated into the normal lecture format. In his lecture analysing the harmonic structure of a Wagner opera at the University of Chichester, the Head of Music and Media, Ben Hall, kept his first year students with him for the full two hours. The room was filled with an eclectic group of 75 students specialising in a wide range of music, from classical, to jazz, and pop, and somehow he presented a lecture that they all followed. He did this without stopping to ask students if they found the content accessible. As he spoke, he used rhetorical devices, like simile and metaphor to bring the complex harmonies closer to the students and humour to keep them engaged. The lecture was presented from his point of view as the teacher, but also as if he was the one learning, so he would verbally explain his thought processes of how and why he understood the material. He linked this discussion to an experience for the students, cleverly integrated their participation by asking them to respond actively, yet in a non-threatening way, to questions. Finding a way for non-invasive participation was essential to the success of the learning, because in a large lecture setting if students are suddenly asked, 'Do you understand?' usually a silence will fall. Nobody wants to admit that they do not understand, as they would be exposed and that would be quite a negative experience. Ben Hall used a small physical gesture that could be kept private, or shared with the instructor; he asked the students to raise an eyebrow to show their understanding.

Case study 3.1: Encouraging active participation

After introducing a musical harmony in detail and explaining its relevance to the opera, Ben Hall asked the 75 students to make it known when they heard the harmony in the music. The task was framed as something that could be a safe, discrete communication between the teacher and student, something that even the person sitting in next chair would not see. Students were asked to test it out and to 'raise one eyebrow in an inquisitive manner' to see if they could indeed be discrete. Hall raised his eyebrow, joining in, and it was silly, which meant that people began to smile. The class then applied this small physical motion when listening to the opera, and the interaction became fun even though they were learning about something very serious and fundamental to the music. This specific eyebrow-raising musical concept was woven throughout the lecture, and Hall would occasionally include his own, art-connoisseur-type eyebrow-raise while introducing and discussing other related examples, to reinforce and remind students of the process of recognising and applying this musical device to different settings within the opera.

Throughout the two-hour lecture, Ben Hall modelled learning for them. The students felt involved in the lecture because of the way the spoken word was presented, almost as a dialogue where both sides were taken by the speaker, and by the use of questioning that highlighted aspects of the learning process that they could actively engage with during the presentation. The ways modelling can inform self-efficacy is discussed in detail in Chapter 4.

Taking it further: Interaction with 1000?

Professor Michael Sandel's lectures at Harvard University have been attended by huge numbers of students. He has taught a single cohort of over 1000 students, and his lectures have extended beyond the four walls of a physical room to reach students in other countries via electronic means. His methodology integrates students into the learning process and allows the lectures to be shaped by that interaction, despite the large size. He embeds certain fundamental qualities of personal interaction into the lecture, and this enables the students to become active participants in their learning and take responsibility for their ideas. After presenting an issue or a point he asks the audience to come forward with specific examples that are either for or against the issue, and asks people to include reasons for their views. Importantly, Sandel asks for everyone's name when they speak and in return, he addresses each speaker by name. He has also been known to include the whole audience by asking for a show of hands to collect opinions on an issue, and then he eloquently knits these different viewpoints together throughout the discussion.

His lecture at the London School of Economics (LSE) was part of the BBC Radio 4 series *Michael Sandel: The Public Philosopher* (Sandel, 2014) and tackled the topic of voting. It was broadcast on 20 May 2014, a few weeks before elections were held in Great Britain, and the engagement from the students on the topic was genuine. Students freely contributed opinions, and beyond providing an answer to questions, they were drawn into the process of debate with Professor Sandel and with one another:

'What's your name?'

'Kirsten'

'What would you say to Colin and Juliet and others who gave principle reasons for not voting? Speak directly ... let's have Colin stand up ... Stand up ... Speak directly to Colin ...' (Sandel, 2014)

This was a particularly poignant moment in the lecture, not because of the content, but because of the methods used to orchestrate the discussion and the learning. In this particular lecture on voting it was not clear where the discussion would go after Kirsten began to speak, and there was a real element of freedom in the session, since the students genuinely supplied some of the content. Professor Sandel acted as a guide for the students during learning. In an interview with LooSE TV after his 2012 lectures at the LSE were recorded for radio, he described the process, 'We did two lectures, and they weren't really lectures, they were interactive discussions' (LooSE TV, 2012).

Looking at Sandel's style in more detail, with relation to student involvement and self-efficacy, he empowers the students, supporting them, validating their beliefs, and creating opportunities for them to gain experience where their thoughts are valued and they can communicate successfully.

How many students would readily volunteer to speak out in a lecture hall of 1000 or even 500 of their peers? Many lecturers promote a culture of submissive silence, but Professor Sandel has cultivated a culture of discussion, and students have come to expect participation. His students are active and demonstrate their self-efficacy by willingly standing up in front of him and the audience and becoming a part of the philosophical debate.

He also integrated the same format of a discussion in his 2010 and 2013 TED talks by making audience comments integral, and he opened his largest lecture, attended by some 15,000 students at Yonsei University, Seoul, South Korea (Ramstad, 2012), by saying, 'We are here for a philosophy lecture, but not just a lecture, also a discussion. Here in the open air. Are you ready to participate with me in a discussion?' (Yonseienglish, 2012). Sandel creates an open environment, inviting both sides of any story, and this allows for great interpersonal differences, yet still individuals can maintain and develop a strong self-efficacy for their capabilities to personally contribute and learn.

Regardless of the group size, learners need to feel and believe that they are invited to participate in their learning. Teachers can act as the guide and catalyst by examining their own practices and becoming aware of how physical interaction, dialogue, and written feedback can influence student understanding. Any small changes that a teacher can introduce into daily routines and interactions to convey and reinforce this to students will help to facilitate the active co-engagement that encourages good communication, learning, and a positive sense of self-belief.

4 Embedding the foundations of self-efficacy in the classroom

Students' perspectives, beliefs, and processes are considered in relation to how they approach learning new concepts and material. Educational and psychological models of learning are discussed and the interrelationships of self-efficacy beliefs within learning process are presented. Various types of modelling, from mastery to student models, are introduced as mechanisms to facilitate understanding and learning, and ways for teachers to integrate these into daily practice are introduced.

To gain entry into higher education, students gain experience from a variety of preparatory experiences, from taking foundational or other courses that build knowledge and experience, passing required tests, and completing interviews and applications required for their specific course. The skills needed and used in their chosen professions, whether engineering, business, catering, may be very different to those used in the classroom for learning theoretical material, and distinguishing these is essential for creating secure self-efficacy beliefs and patterns for successful learning. Reading textbooks, essay writing, and revising are all far removed from the on-the-job application of a good bedside manner by a nurse practitioner. The understanding of how to learn is not automatic, and then taking the learning and applying and connecting it to practical skill use is again another process. A student who is naturally confident in practical matters may still find challenges with aspects of the learning process. Misaligning judgement beliefs can cause problems for students, whether they are over or under confident.

▶ Learning: Skills, techniques, and content

A strong sense of self-efficacy has been shown to affect choices, predict engagement, and, ultimately, reflect levels of attainment (Bandura, 1993; Zimmerman, 2000; Linnenbrink & Pintrich, 2003). A combination of seen and unseen, external and internal, physical and psychological factors all contribute to students' understanding of their capabilities. Individuals rely on their own perceptions of how developed their skills are, assessing their practical achievements and experiences and supporting these judgements with any external benchmarks such as awards or qualifications they have achieved. These past experiences are considered alongside interactions with others, personal attributes, and aspects of the current situation, along with the values and expectations that surround the task itself; these aspects all influence forming self-efficacy judgements when approaching learning.

Belief

When students approach a new task, there are a host of influences on their self-efficacy beliefs, including understanding the task itself. The way students perceive control over learning processes affects their sense of ownership over both learning and achievement. If students believe that progress is not because of their own skills, understanding, and capabilities, but is actually a reflection or 'halo effect' coming from the teacher's direct involvement (McPherson & Schubert, 2004), then even if those learning experiences are positive, they will have little impact on building or reinforcing the students' self-beliefs. Whenever students believe that what they have done is not something that came from them, whether it is a positive or negative experience, that event is less likely to significantly affect their self-efficacy for carrying out the actual task. This is also true of situations where students believe the outcome is because of some other uncontrollable circumstance or luck (Cleary & Zimmerman, 2001). Either success or failure can be attributed to causes beyond the individual's control. For example, if a student won an art competition and does not believe that his or her work was skilled or creative, but that other entries were particularly poor, or if an exam failure resulted from the whole class being moderated down, or because someone was late because the train was cancelled, these are instances when the student defers ownership of the experience and the result to something external and not to his or her own capabilities. Sometimes this is correct, and in other settings it can be from a lack of understanding or a skewed perception of learning.

As students develop, perceptions of who and what can influence their learning also changes. Early in schooling children attribute success to effort and hard work (Austin, Renwick, & McPherson, 2006), but as they grow there is more of an understanding of skills and their own cognitive processes. It is not necessary that successful learning experiences always have to be effortful, as people also learn from reflection and observation of those around them (Brockbank & McGill, 2007). Both people directly involved with learning and those on the periphery of an experience impact a student's views. Social pressures and acceptance can be influential throughout different periods of life. In times of change like adolescence, people look to others for examples to use as they make and confirm judgements about themselves

(Pintrich & Schunk, 2002), as they are still developing their sense of self and sometimes doubt in their own capabilities to adequately make these judgements (Schunk & Meece, 2006).

There is not a definitive cut-off as to when social influences begin or end, and the value given to various people's opinions changes throughout education, as students gain expertise and their own accomplishments (Pajares & Schunk, 2001; Cleary & Zimmerman, 2001). Social groups can be powerful influences in students' lives, but only if the students allow this and continue to value these external judgements over their own. When people consider their capabilities in relation to their personal potential and not in terms of outside influences or benchmarks, then they break free from the reliance on social contexts for comparisons and begin to take responsibility for their self-beliefs.

Symptoms of low self-efficacy

An important aspect of making a self-efficacy judgement that is reliable and accurate has to do with understanding the nature of the task (Bandura, 1997; Bong, 2006). Understanding the specific criteria and type of skills that are needed for learning can inform an accurate judgement about their self-efficacy for learning. Pajares (1996b) advised that self-efficacy for learning should be assessed before the task is carried out, as a starting point, and as the task continues and the student does learn and progress, this will influence and change his or her self-efficacy for learning beliefs. A clear picture of these beliefs is useful at the outset of learning, as it relates to engagement, motivation, choice, and can give a teacher an indication of which students might need help or clarification of the tasks and methods they should use in learning.

Past experiences also influence a student's beliefs when approaching new projects, with positive experiences effectively building self-efficacy beliefs and negative experiences bringing them down. For something to have an impact, first there must be an awareness of the accomplishment. It may not be intuitive for students to separate and recognise progress in learning as an accomplishment while still working towards a larger, or more final, goal. With every task there is the learning and then the delivery or performance of the task. Assessments produce obvious outcomes, such as exam results, but the week-on-week learning can be overlooked and not recognised as a separate task. Students may not realise that their progress in learning, as they develop and use skills, is a positive accomplishment and can very much contribute to how they view their capabilities apply the knowledge in assessments. Helping students to interpret their progress within learning by highlighting their progressive achievements will build their self-efficacy beliefs.

When students do not consider learning a task, which is made of layers of separate methods and skills, they may skip over these and solely focus on carrying out the final assessment. Imagine that a student is awarded a low-average grade on an essay exam. Without taking into account how he or she approached learning, he or she might practically (but incorrectly) attribute the low achievement directly to the criteria or skill requirements of the task itself: being bad at writing essays or not performing well in an exam setting. The student may indeed be weak in pressurised assessments, but it is also possible that the student was not accomplished in efficient learning, and this was revealed in the assessment setting. This view is skewed and will misinform the student's self-efficacy beliefs that are built from that assessment experience. Learning is an essential precursor task to doing well in the exam, but it is separate from taking the exam. Recognising progress in accomplishment is valuable for students to form accurate self-efficacy judgements.

The results from exams or coursework will inform self-efficacy views, but these beliefs are not a direct result of the marks. It is possible to have a good result that does not have a great impact and to have a negative experience that is not very damaging to that person's self-efficacy. Understanding the processes that contribute to the moment of delivery can make the task less daunting and can dissolve much of a negative experience.

When students have a new task to approach and they say they are worried or not confident, ask them to consider why. Are they underprepared? Is there some danger involved? It is a teacher's role to unravel any unfounded low self-efficacy beliefs. If when the worry is discussed students can see that they have prepared, do understand the task, and are ready to do as well as they physically and mentally can, then there are simply less grounds for having doubt and the negative self-efficacy beliefs should become more positive. This is more than using verbal persuasion from the teacher, because although the teacher may present the argument, it is backed up with experiential evidence of the student's preparation.

If students are aware that they have had past difficulties, for example with research skills or with note taking, then this will impact the way they approach new work that also uses these skills. With low self-efficacy students may attempt to avoid the task, making sure they do not experience failure (Bandura, 1997; Bensimon, 2007). Sometimes external pressures affect the person's self-efficacy. There may be time constraints with external work or personal commitments, and these can influence the way the student approaches tasks either positively or negatively. One person might be overwhelmed whereas another will find the same situation an exciting challenge.

It is far less likely that students in higher education will be completely unfamiliar with their chosen subject areas and the tasks they will undertake, but there is still an element of the unknown and of newness when entering higher education. It is a reality that students need guidance to understand the nature of learning and assessment throughout their courses. A greater degree of autonomy is expected as students progress, and learning may also simply be different from what was previously experienced in school or college settings. The challenges that first come with taking learning out of the textbook and into practical applications should not be underestimated. Without a clear vision of how and what the student will do, learning in higher education can be daunting.

Process

Scholars and psychologists have described learning processes with various diagrams and flow charts, yet there are slight differences in the way ideas are presented in different subject areas. Today, educators agree that learning is a process (Kolb, 1984, p.38) and not simply something that happens to students. In a larger framework, learning is situated both alongside and within Bandura's (1986) cycle of human interaction, with fluid and interdependent relationships between the personal, environmental, and behavioural elements in everyday happenings. Texts aimed at specialists in education do not cite the same models as those written for psychologists, and this is not uncommon that the same concept is addressed with slightly different terminology in unrelated subject areas, and yet other concepts exist in multiple domains but do not have specific terminology. For example, in music when a performer has issues with nerves this is called performance anxiety, but when they perform well there is no particular term for this. Colloquially musicians refer to being 'in the zone', however, in sport this is facilitative anxiety (Hanton & Jones 1999; Hanton, O'Brien, & Mellalieu, 2003). Using different terminology to describe the same situation does not imply that it does not exist in one field, or that a particular name for the mechanisms within learning processes is more correct than another. Each teacher must sift through the learning theories and terminology embedded within his or her specialism to find wider relationships and to draw out what is specifically relevant and useful to everyday practice and everyday development. Even though the crossover of terminology is not consistent between educational and research contexts, it is important to focus on the central, core aspects to find relevance in both research and teaching practices across subject areas.

Below are a few conceptual ideas about learning, drawn from both education and psychology, that lead to a useful understanding of where self-efficacy fits within the theoretical context and how it impacts learning.

The model of Experiential Learning presented by Kolb 'combines experience, perception, cognition, and behaviour' (Kolb, 1984, p.21). In his model, the student experiences something, reflects on observations, forms an understanding of what happened, and then actively implements what was learned. This is often then depicted in the form of a spiral, illustrating a continuum of learning built on experience. The principle that learning is an active process is fundamental, and Kolb's model stresses the active, personal, and progressive aspects of learning.

Cowan (2006) builds on the Kolb cycle by integrating various types of reflection as presented by Schön (1987) into a model of learning. He observes that students have experiences, but that the reflection sometimes happens at different points within the learning process. Reflection can occur during the active process of carrying out a task, and at other times; because of the practicalities of a task someone cannot pause mid-flow, and the reflection happens retrospectively. For example, in performance disciplines where the action must unfold, the student cannot necessarily stop the music, dance, or game to reflect. In Cowan's model there are elaborate spin-off loops representing different types of reflection during or after learning. The effect is to transform Kolb's spiral into something more like calligraphy. It is important to acknowledge that students will have unique and possibly complex experiences of learning, that will vary depending on person, subject, and context, and the elaborate nature of the resulting model becomes very subject specific.

Schunk (2000) recognises that the experience of learning is broader than enactive engagement in the beginning of his book *Learning theories: An educational perspective* (p.2) when he quotes Shuell (1986) to define learning.

Learning is an enduring change in behaviour, or in the capacity to behave in a given fashion, which results from practice or other forms of experience. (Schuell, 1986, p. 412)

These other forms of experience can include modelled behaviour and vicarious learning. In his Social Learning Theory, Bandura (1977) explains how people can learn from observing those around them. These types of learning do not replace actual experiences, but the learner can make connections and draw meaning from observational learning. There are considerable areas where aspects of the different theories begin to complement one another and even sometimes overlap, and Kolb himself says that his ideas are very close to Bandura's social cognitive view (Kolb, 1984, p.36). Kolb (1984) called this process – translating and reflecting on experiences to make meaningful connections with the content – the "abstract conceptualisation of learning".

Zimmerman's (1989) learning cycle expands on these models by adding a stage before the active, or observed, learning experience begins. Before learning, students formulate expectations through forethought by analysing what they know about the learning and consider how ready and willing they are to learn. Zimmerman's learning cycle begins with this stage and moves into the active part of learning, where learners have control over their experience, and after the experience there is a third stage of reflection on what happened. He discusses cognitive processes and includes these alongside externally visible activity as valid experiences within the active stage of learning. Both the student who imagines riding a bicycle and the one who physically climbs on and cycles down the road are having learning experiences. One is achieved through mental activity and the other is physically engaged. There are many ways to learn and formulate meaningful understandings of what is experienced. Developing learning and fostering self-efficacy happen when students make good use of what happens in the less outwardly visible stages that happen before and after the learning.

Zimmerman (2002) also differentiates naïve and experienced learners, and stresses that less-experienced learners tend to react to learning instead of preparing effectively through forethought. In the forethought stage, students use their existing knowledge and experience to form self-efficacy beliefs, making judgements about their capabilities for the tasks ahead. Self-efficacy is pivotal throughout learning and informs how students view and choose their learning goals, the strategies they use, and the way they approach difficulties. The meaning that students attribute to their learning in reflection then feeds their self-efficacy beliefs, creating a cycle of constant influence. When these beliefs are strong and positively reinforced, their attitude towards learning, engagement, and progress will also grow, but when students are full of doubt and self-efficacy is low, then similarly, this can become a negative spiral. The way students engage with forethought and reflection can result in deeper, more meaningful learning.

Students often make a jump when entering the higher education system, where learning is more demanding and requires both more complexity of thought and ownership of process than in previous school settings. Unless the tasks are direct duplicates of what students have already experienced, there is no reason teachers should assume that students already know how to approach new learning tasks effectively. Teachers have been criticised for not teaching processes, and institutions for not developing independent learners (Jørgensen, 2000). Teachers are aware that more explanation needs to be presented within a practical context (Triantafyllaki, 2005), but this can become difficult in lecture settings with very large groups. From a teacher's perspective, being aware of learning processes and how mental and physical factors interact to form the student's perception of his or her capabilities and readiness to learn can help teachers guide students in choosing strategies to enable effective learning.

... thinking about it

▶ When did you learn to learn?
▶ As a student were you aware of your learning processes?
▶ What keeps you aware of these processes now?

▶ Demonstrating student understanding

Learning and building beliefs is a multifaceted process, and a teacher can only know a small part of what the student experiences, but an ongoing dialogue between the teacher and student creates openness and allows for collaboration. Inviting student interaction is not limited here to an exchange of a few words after a lecture or in a tutorial setting. The teacher can guide and confirm any stage of the learning process if communication with the student is open and fluid. Creating situations where a dialogue exists between student and teacher, and both provide elements of the input and responses, are integral parts of the learning process.

Interactive teaching can reinforce and develop positive learning experiences through student participation. When working together, the teacher can present questions that encourage the students' reflection and understanding to find new strategies or explore different methods in their learning. Questioning can take on many different forms, and although as a method it can seem extremely simple, questioning is not primarily a technique for finding a particular 'right' answer. Asking questions that are open-ended primers encourages and teaches the student to look within and think, analyse, and create, and this can lead to developing deeper learning and fostering self-efficacy beliefs.

Questions do several things for the student. They instigate thought about the subject, and on the simplest level, questions require a reply. This is also a way to invite and engage students who are not openly willing to participate in their learning. Sometimes this begins with the student becoming aware that the question itself may present something new that the student may never have considered. From the teacher's point of view, there needs to be a judgement-free environment that allows and welcomes student discovery and exploration.

Leading questions can also have the pleasant consequence of producing answers, but more importantly, they open the door for students to discover new ideas for themselves. Through a series of directed questions, the teacher can progressively guide students through the steps necessary to understand an issue. Verbally articulating students' mental and physical processes externalises the learning and makes it tangible. Through this, and without realising it, students begin to be taught the stepping stones of how to self-regulate their learning. Creating the patterns that make a habit of awareness requires patience from the teacher, as each student will be slightly different in approach, needs, and understanding.

Case study: Hans Jensen

The cello teacher Hans Jensen is always looking for his students to think and search for their own answers to questions. Jensen always asks his students questions about their cello playing. What did you think? What would you like to change? How do you do that? How is this phrase different? Of course, this questioning is not a lack of knowledge on his part, nor is he particularly looking to find an articulated verbal answer to a question. It is his way of accomplishing several things from a teaching standpoint: he invites communication and reflection. It allows him to gain a confirmation of what the students understand, what aspects of the task they are actively considering, and whether they are aware of either processes or outcomes. Simply observing people as they learn or perform a task gives part of that picture, but the internal aspects, the thoughts and planning, and awareness of how processes manifest themselves through physical delivery are not necessarily observable. These gaps between the student experience and the teacher's perception can be partially addressed through an active dialogue.

Professor Jensen answers students' questions, but wherever possible he brings the conversation back to the student, so students do not look to him for an easy or definite fix for challenges they face in learning, but look inwardly, reflecting and drawing upon the knowledge and skills they already have. This dialogue creates a situation where the students feel free to ask questions. Some students are so hungry for answers, and when they keep asking for more and more answers, Jensen will deflect the questions back on to them, to avoid a sense of dependency and encourage students to take responsibility for their learning.

Although any student can feel stranded when direct answers aren't given, Jensen never leaves his students without guidance. He expects his students to be responsible: to actively listen, to fully engage with ideas. He leads with directed questions, challenging students to search for methods to change,

Case study 4.1: Questioning and promoting student thinking

A student once asked this very direct question: "When I practise the music should I be playing this slowly or in the final speed?"

Jensen is a very charismatic personality and answered with a challenging reply, but presented it with enthusiasm:

"You have the answer: both! *You* have to do it to find out. Try all the possibilities and then you need to figure out when each works. *I* don't have the answers. You have to figure it out. [pause] How do you want it to sound?"

The student replied, slightly concerned, "I don't know?"

Jensen smiled and encouraged the student, "You don't have to know yet. You're trying different things. When you perform it you will have to know, but you are learning it now."

enhance, or improve their current practice. Having that balance where students remain receptive is not easy and 'great delicacy is needed if critical feedback is to have the effect of helping students, especially inexperienced ones, to learn something rather than to become defensive or disheartened' (Ramsden, 2003, p.188). Jensen keeps this openness by respecting student suggestions, listening to their ideas and genuinely testing them out with the same rigour and respect as any of his ideas.

This dialogue of questions does not represent the end of a single closed process, but it is the beginning of an extended cycle of exploring ideas. Jensen will move on to suggest another parameter in that student's music making to change, perhaps something technical. For example, he may ask about the way loudness or softness is achieved on the cello during a specific passage in the music. When a student puts forward a good idea, Jensen will validate it and encourage it with further questions to explain how he or she could continue to develop the idea and use it to make more progress. After exploring series of possibilities for any challenging situation, from both the student and teacher, he and the student will discuss how to choose a solution that works well. Then the student reflects, and forms an abstract concept (Kolb, 1984) of the idea that works best so there is an intellectual understanding. After exploring that suggestion, he would reinforce the process and encourage the student to try it again so the student could then take it in and begin to make a judgement on whether it was something he or she indeed wanted to do. This is then applied to that student's work, so it can be integrated into practice in a way that personally, physically, and musically works for that individual.

His students are being taught the processes of how to think and solve complex problems for themselves, and this methodology works very well both in the one-to-one setting of music lessons and in the group setting of teaching his studio class of 15–20 students. There is a strong element of trust between the teacher and the students and there is an awareness that the process is *for* the students, not something external that is being imposed upon them. As students become more proficient in examining their processes and tasks through questioning, they will contribute suggestions and become more comfortable initiating ideas and exploring possibilities in discussion. This allows and encourages an open-minded approach to both learning and, eventually, to performing.

When learning in any discipline there is always the possibility for questioning: How is the project progressing compared to your original plan? Do you like the look of what you have made and will someone else look at it in the same way? Why does the text read so well in that passage? There is no limit to the amount of improvement or the level of detail that can be explored within any given topic. It depends on the awareness of the student, the focus, the level, the goals, the repertoire the list can go on infinitely within each area of specialisation. There is a complex web between learning and intrapersonal interaction, and individual circumstances will determine how far questioning and developing any given aspect or a task is taken with each individual student.

When students become aware in questioning, they begin to engage with the forethought stage of learning. Over time and with experience, student perceptions will become more acute and they will expand their approach to considering new ideas. This will encourage students to explore their learning processes, giving them more experience with a wider range of cognitive strategies, and when ideas are translated and integrated into the students' work, they can take responsibility for their achievement.

▶ Exploring modelling: Creating safe experiences

Teachers have a privileged role allowing them to invite students to learn, experience, think, and believe. Learning and experience shape self-efficacy beliefs, and once created these beliefs become part of the fabric that makes individuals who they are. To ensure students' experiences are directed to enable success is paramount. This does not imply teachers should manufacture experiences that are unrealistically easy to guarantee success, but that the tools, methods, and opportunities are there for students to engage with and use. The teacher's role in modelling ranges from being a facilitator to a role that is often active, and sometimes teachers do experience moments of vulnerability when demonstrating learning processes. However, a transparent involvement in modelling learning to students is a powerful tool for learning, as subject matter and content are made real for those observing.

Many teachers include demonstrated examples during their teaching, and the way these are carried out can result in profoundly different impacts on students' perceptions, attitudes, and beliefs. Key aspects of the learning process that separate the naïve from more experienced learners are internal. Both the planning and analysis of forethought and the reassessment and realignment of goals that happen in reflection are generally unseen by the teacher, and considering this makes presenting clear demonstrations to students more important so they can meaningfully interpret the content for themselves. In higher education the student is expected to do more and more independently, and teachers can use modelling to present and encourage goals by example (Finkel & Fitzsimons, 2011). When students observe, it is an opportunity for vicarious types of experiences to take place. If students are able to make the connections between themselves and observed actions, then the knowledge from that experience can be directly added to their repertoire, and influence how they personally approach similar tasks. However, if the model or their actions are too far from the understanding of the observer, then the transferability of the demonstration and its application may simply go unnoticed. The following discussion of modelling focuses on the active part within learning, and the reflection and forethought will be outlined in detail in Chapter 5 with a discussion of self-regulated learning behaviours.

If students have robust senses of self-efficacy they will strive to find and make connections with any observed material, despite the model. A driven student will find strength and inspiration even in differences, and will seek ways to use aspects of a demonstration that may be very far above or below his or her current experience or performance level. There is an element that these students can and will make progress because a strong sense of self-belief in their learning capabilities carries them forward. If students are less assured and have low self-efficacy, then in order for the model to be influential, a direct and obviously non-threatening connection needs to be presented in a way that does not challenge the students' delicate self-beliefs.

As students progress, they need less input from modelled situations, but in the early stages of learning, a scaffolded approach where teachers offer support and show how tasks are done can greatly improve students' approach to carrying out tasks and the results they achieve (Schunk & Zimmerman, 1997, 2007).

Throughout the learning process, although less direct input is needed, students may still need to revisit notes and texts about the core concepts involved in what they are doing, especially as they explore the layers of a task and realise the challenges of applying skills to a situation for themselves (Schunk, 1998). Bandura (1977) outlines four critical stages to achieving effective modelling:

► Attention
► Retention
► Reproduction
► Reinforcement and motivation

Attention

Exposing students to modelled situations does not automatically mean that they will relate the demonstration to their future practice or in fact learn anything from it. Different aspects of a modelled situation will resonate with individual students, and Bandura highlights that a model with 'winsome' characteristics will be more readily observed than someone who performs equally well but does not have the same personable qualities (Bandura, 1977). That is not to say that the demonstrator needs to be a particularly beautiful sort of model, but that the presentation qualities, from aspects of appearance to the method of speaking, including tone, pace, and inflection, as well as facial and physical gestures, can all impact the student or audience reception of the demonstration. For modelling to be effective, the students need to be aware of the specific processes that are being demonstrated, the strategies that are used, and of how this relates to them. Processes can be introduced and defined through literature and in theoretical contexts, but students must engage with that material before they can learn from it. Teachers can draw upon what is familiar to students by using aspects of common student behaviour and interaction, as opposed to presenting situations that are far removed from something a student could readily associate with to create effective modelled situations.

Retention

When observing a modelled experience, the students create a representational understanding of what they see; effectively they are making a memory. To affect their own learning and development, they must be able to then recall the experience and reflect on it sometime after they leave that class setting. Bandura stipulates that translating the experience into both an image map and some form of verbal coding can produce effective longer-term learning (1977, p.7). This also relates to Kolb's (1984) stage of forming abstract conceptualisations of the learned material. It makes sense that a stronger link with the memory will be formed if the observed experience is reinforced, and the processes of thinking through to analyse and code what was seen does this. There is a difference between watching a performance or film for enjoyment and watching to understand the craft and delivery of the acting and understanding the content on an analytical level. If student-observers watch with deliberate and focused attention, they can also form links with other areas of their knowledge and experience. Making a mental record of events, having in-class or online discussions, and written descriptions or notes all assist the student to review, reflect on, and access processes within the specific scenario demonstrated to them.

Reproduction

Recreating the learned behaviours depends largely on how effectively the retention stage has been executed. Imitating what has been observed is valuable for students and allows them to begin to reflect on the meaning of what they have seen (Schön, 1987; Brockbank & McGill, 2007). The students' ability to perform what they observed is also heavily reliant on whether they have mastered the skills necessary to do so. If they are aiming to operate a complex machine, they must first understand the technicalities of how to do that activity and actually acquire the skills. Without the necessary skills, attempted reproduction is only mimicry, and the lack of understanding will be exposed as soon as any unpredicted factors complicate the situation. Even when students are well equipped to carry out the task themselves, a physical task takes more than mental understanding. Observation does not replace the deliberate practice required to gain skill. Learning requires initial experimentation, and depending on how complicated the task is there may be layers of learning and small activities needed before the student can reproduce the modelled behaviour with confidence and security. Initial attempts often require corrections, and when students feel supported and free to explore these processes, they are more likely to work towards success. In a practical setting, this is why it is so important for the learning environment to be safe and nurturing.

Reinforcement and motivation

Anything new can challenge or stretch what students consider comfortable, because they may feel exposed and not yet confident. Providing a positive setting for students to put the observed behaviours into practice will encourage them. Reinforcement in terms of validating what students are doing will enable them to continue to develop what was modelled, instead of leaving the knowledge as a safely understood yet untested concept. Especially with students, this final step of giving them that nudge that says 'yes, I believe in you' and encourages them to take the step to explore and put new ideas into practice is very necessary. Without this, the students can be aware and understand, but before they have actually done it for themselves, they still can have that element of doubt that perhaps they cannot do it.

Drawing upon the different sources that influence self-efficacy, the model is a vicarious influence, and this can be supplemented by the verbal reassurance of the teacher. Then when the student begins to master the behaviour, teachers can ensure that there is reinforcement so that it is a positive experience. Students do not have to be on their own throughout this process. There are various types of modelling that can be used at different points of the student's learning.

Mastery model

When presenting a *mastery model*, the activity is carried out with ease and precision; the person demonstrating is in control of the task and it is polished as if in a professional setting. Few people regularly present their teaching with a level of pre-planned and rehearsed detail seen in a documentary; teachers are not often comfortable presenting anything less than a convincing mastery model for their students. Teachers are less likely to fumble and make overt mistakes, unless this is a planned part of the presentation. A mastery model allows for a correct and efficient demonstration that uses well-developed skills and presents a clean, clear display of the task or situation for students. However good this may be, it is not always the most helpful for students. Students with weak self-efficacy will attempt to make direct comparisons and associate with a professional demonstration, and they see their own lack of skill and are aware of the (perceived) gaping differences between their abilities and the goal of replicating the demonstration on their own. They may not even be able to imagine how they could ever get from their current state of understanding to the level needed to carry out the task as well as the teacher, and this can cause people to quit before they begin the learning process. A perfect model will allow a teacher to present his or her own skill in a good light, but can act as a deterrent to students and actually impede their learning.

There are appropriate times to have a flawless demonstration, and it is important to demonstrate the professionalism and currency of the teacher's skill. Practically, a mastery model can positively influence students in the final stages of learning, as they prepare to demonstrate their skills in an assessed, or public, performance setting. In the later stages of learning, the student will be more skilled, and closing the gap between the student's skill level to that of the model will seem reachable. When the teacher is confident the student will positively associate with a mastery model, then a well-delivered presentation by a model can inspire and positively motivate the student to polish their skills and achieve more.

Case study 4.2: Progressive modelling for medical students

Mr Mark Pemberton is Faculty at the Royal College of Surgeons and incorporates modelling into his teaching when training medical students to be surgeons. Just as students in other disciplines learn about methods in their university lectures, medical students study procedures and the specific steps needed to plan these actions. The methods and their details are explained many times to students. They then go to theatre to observe them in practice, reinforcing their learning and allowing them to see these under live conditions. It is not practical for students to perform complex procedures on live patients before they are qualified and have the necessary experience. They observe the professionals who have mastered the tasks working precisely and demonstrating fluency. To bridge the gap between their understanding of theory and practical applications, students also have the opportunity to get closer and take an active part in theatre work. When this happens, their role is discussed in detail and agreed upon before the procedure, and clear parameters are set. It is important that students remain interested throughout and not frustrated by the experience, as sometimes medical procedures take several hours. So if a student is managing the light for the surgeon or holding the thread during sewing, even though these may seem small jobs, the student is involved in the process, and is no longer only an observer. Even these small tasks must be carried out with precision so the overall task can be a success.

The experience is all planned, and that way the student's engagement is safe, with the professional still in control. It is geared to allow the student to achieve a successful experience. Later in training, as graduates and junior doctors, there are a series of roles that students progressively take on, allowing them to gradually increase their responsibility and confidence in the professional arena.

Coping model

When the teacher fully demonstrates the processes involved in carrying out a task, including potential pitfalls, the cognitive processes, and the choices that are made about methods and actions, this is a *coping model* (Schunk, 1981). A coping demonstration is not intended to be a perfect performance, and it should make any difficulties clearly visible, so students can observe the way the teacher uses various strategies to negotiate challenges within the task. The 'working out' is made evident and appears to expose the presenter as weak through failing to instantly or easily achieve success, but it is this that enables students to make links to themselves. A coping model allows students to see someone go through the difficulties of learning and perservere to the end. This can act as a very positive teaching tool and break the barrier of untouchable perfection that a professional presentation can have, to make the path of learning more clear and approachable for the student. With a sample of students in higher education, Zimmerman and Kitsantas (2002) found that a coping model was more effective than a mastery model, and students particularly benefitted from having specific information about how to correct the problems they would encounter in their learning. The person demonstrating can verbally describe what is happening, as if an aural annotation of self-thoughts, to highlight where choices need to be made and specific skills that students will use. Schunk and Hanson (1989) used a further form of modelling with this verbalisation that they called the *coping–emotive* model. In this setting there are verbalisations that illustrate initial doubt in capabilities and acknowledge the task difficulty that accompany the demonstration. With children, it was found that this *emotive* model produced the biggest increase in their self-efficacy for learning.

Teacher modelling

Teachers are used to standing in front of students and explaining, but they need to choose carefully how they present any scenario to students. A teacher is not always the easiest person for a student to relate to, and demonstrating in a way that illustrates the challenges of a task can seem awkward or contrived, as students have an expectation that the teacher is knowledgeable and can also carry out the tasks being taught with ease and fluency. This gives rise to the reason why a teacher may not always be the best model to show the struggles and challenges that students find when first attempting a task. It can be extremely awkward when the teacher goes against expectations if the student is not aware of what is happening.

   Students and teachers both make assumptions; there is a challenge to navigating these expectations, and they impact the reception and reaction people have to different types of modelled situation. I demonstrate this predicament with a class of final year music students who are preparing to start their own private teaching practices. When the class arrives, the room is set out for a musical performance and the students sit in rows, with notebooks and tablets ready for the session. I then enter the room with my cello and take my seat in front of them. All eyes rest quietly on me as the students wait for me to perform. After placing my music on the stand, and dropping a few pages on the floor, I begin to play my cello. Already there is an air of awkwardness and the class is not sure whether I have been careless or disorganised with my music. After only a few seconds of the performance, the students are becoming noticeably uncomfortable. The playing has errors. I stop and go back over a musical phrase that contained wrong notes and even practice self-talk to help myself correct the problem. The effect of my playing wrong notes, stopping mid-flow, and commenting while I work out difficulties is obvious and shocking for the students. They are visibly uncomfortable at seeing a 'professional' not perform well. The students do not realise that I am purposefully demonstrating a coping model, because they have not been prepared for this. Without being ready for what they see and understanding how the demonstration is meant to unfold, the processes can be completely missed and misinterpreted.

The purpose of an imperfect display is not to see the students squirm as they endure the amateurish mistakes, but to give them an illustrative experience of the expectations that students unknowingly place on their teachers. When a teacher models something, simply showing something is not enough. Bandura (1977) stresses that exposure to a modelled situation does not guarantee that there will be attention or learning. For the students to meaningfully comprehend the coping demonstration, there needs to be a discussion to preface the situation and highlight the purpose of how it relates to them and their own practice. A teacher can be a very effective coping model when the premise is set and the students know that the teacher is playing a part, so they can then follow and associate with the role-modelled situation. Playing a part does need to be believable, and if a teacher can support a demonstration with the explanation of the underlying skill and thinking, then exposing process and even the process of working through errors or difficulties does not threaten the teacher's image as a professional, but serves to strengthen the student understanding.

...thinking about it

Mastery and **Coping** models are non-threatening for students, as the student role is mainly to observe. These can act as a point of entry for teachers to introduce modelling and make students more aware of processes.

► Teachers can feel less exposed when demonstrating a coping model if it is made clear that their actions *show processes* and flaws are intended as part of the role, not a reflection of a lack of skill or preparation.

Peer modelling: Removing barriers

There are two types of peer models that can be used. One is where the students knowingly act as a model and demonstrate a task or situation to one another. There needs to be a very encouraging and open atmosphere for students to feel comfortable when standing in front of peers, and competition is often inherent in many learning settings, with grades as a constant reminder of who is best. Schulze and Schulze (2003) point out that 'in a competitive atmosphere, there is little incentive for more competent students to provide assistance for students who are having trouble with a given concept or assignment' (p.108). To effectively model a task and its processes, the student must already have a certain level of understanding, and peer models provide an opportunity for more able students to demonstrate and explain to classmates who may be struggling with the concepts. It can be very daunting for students to be put in a leadership or authoritative position in front of peers where they must be confident in their knowledge and skill use and communicate their thought processes clearly to others. Students can explore modelling in small groups, where the whole class does not watch them, and if several small groups work this way at once there is yet another level of peer modelling among several 'leaders' who are demonstrating at the same time. Overall this experience will strengthen the self-efficacy of the able students who act as models, and where collaborative working and discussion take place, it can also boost the self-efficacy of the struggling students as they relate to and learn from their peers. The situation becomes less about overcoming or surpassing classmates and more about each individual's accomplishments and how he or she progresses in personal learning. Observing a peer can be more effective than watching a teacher model a situation when students find the learning challenging (Alderman, 1999), because direct comparisons between students and a peer are more apparent, making the situation influential for learning and for building self-efficacy beliefs (Schunk, 2003).

Peer modelling can be guided and highlighted by the teacher in ways that do not require the students to feel exposed. When students achieve a particular success, the teacher can use that example, with permission from the student, and this does not require the student to actively demonstrate or take a leadership role in front of peers. The teacher can either present the student's success for them or structure a discussion where the student is interviewed to explain his or her working procedures and draw the other students' attention to the steps taken. The other students see the accomplishment as coming from a fellow student, and having a peer model can be more effective than having a teacher model. With the teacher acting as the mediator to explain the example, the student does not have to perform well or explain effectively. A teacher can explain an example that either demonstrates mastery or coping to accomplish a task. It is very possible that a student picks up a concept very quickly and the teacher would like to use that as an example so that others too might learn in a similar way. Coping models can be teased out through probing questions, and as long as the teacher guides students, a discussion can highlight the positive choices to navigate various challenges. For the student who is the positive example, the analysis of the success will reinforce his or her actions and should in turn motivate more achievement. The other students will be able to sympathise with the struggles, and seeing that they were not insurmountable but could be solved through strategic thinking can be very valuable to hear from another student. The same accomplishments might go unnoticed in a general group-learning environment where there is no specific intention of using modelling. The teacher's involvement here is essential because a step-by-step guided explanation ensures that the process is clearly explained. For new or struggling students this can lead them on from the initial stage of attention, to the other components of modelling: retention, reproduction, and then motivation to continue and use what is learned for themselves.

5 Developing mastery experiences

This chapter focuses on mastery experiences as something that students can personally take responsibility for and achieve. Self-regulation, which allows individuals to incrementally attend to all aspects of their learning, is presented, and associated skills and behaviours are outlined within the various dimensions of self-regulation and their application to academic settings. The relationship of strategic thinking to successful achievement and to developing and reinforcing self-efficacy is explored and positioned as a tool for developing confident, autonomous learners.

Facilitating meaningful, independent experiences for students in higher education, when contact time is so precious, is an art form. Students need to be motivated, manage their resources well, and truly believe in themselves and in what they are doing to make the most of the possibilities presented to them. Psychologists, researchers, and practitioners stress that both skills and beliefs are necessary for successful accomplishments (Collins, 1982; Bandura, 1993; Hofer, Yu, & Pintrich, 1998; Schunk & Pajares, 2009), and educators play a key role in guiding these processes.

When students are aware of their learning environment and the ways they can approach and shape their learning experiences, then they are in a good position to become self-regulated learners. Zimmerman (2002) defines self-regulation as 'the self-directive processes by which learners transform their mental abilities into academic skills' (p.65). Self-regulated learning refers to a context where a person chooses to direct his or her learning activities, physical or mental, towards a goal (Zimmerman, 2000). This includes using a range of strategies, resources, planning, and monitoring throughout learning. When students self-regulate their learning, they are aware of their situation and how they control and approach their learning; being passive is not part of that process. People who take charge and self-regulate their learning tend to exhibit many of the same positive qualities, such as using strategic thinking, persisting through challenges, and higher attainment, as people with high self-efficacy (Bandura, 1997; Zimmerman, 2000). On a practical level, the interrelationship of self-efficacy and self-regulated learning gives insight into how both those who study and teach can engage with effective, productive learning that leads to successful results.

In the beginning stages of learning, student behaviours lack the complexity and resourcefulness needed to direct learning independently, and there can be a heavy reliance on teachers' input in order to progress (Hallam, 2001; McPherson & Renwick, 2001). Self-regulation and strategic learning may not be intuitive to all students, but these skills and processes can be developed and taught (Zimmerman, 2002). Educational studies have shown learning about self-regulation helps students who are less experienced learners, and the use of skills in more advanced students is enhanced through further instruction (Risemberg & Zimmerman, 1992; Zimmerman, 2002). Self-efficacy and self-regulated learning have a close relationship, informing and affecting one another throughout learning. When people adopt self-regulated learning strategies they also develop and strengthen the qualities associated with self-efficacious people; there is a reciprocal relationship between self-efficacy and self-regulated learning. People with high self-efficacy tend to adopt more complex self-regulated learning strategies, which in turn enhance the learning process and allow for greater accomplishments (Zimmerman & Martinez-Pons, 1990; Schunk & Pajares, 2009).

With self-regulation, students take an active role in initiating, choosing, and carrying out learning, as opposed to following a predetermined path and reacting to set, external instruction. The strategies students adopt depend on their resourcefulness and capability for engaging with cognitive processes; if students either do not understand or are not proficient with a method, they are unlikely to use it. Progress can be more efficient when the learner is open to allowing for change and is sensitive to the course of learning so strategies can be adapted to best suit each individual setting. Without ingenuity, a student could carry out the teacher's instructions in rote-type learning or attempt to approach an assignment in a purely linear manner, even though this is not the most effective way to learn. Ritchie and Kearney (2013) observed naïve learners who approached learning new musical repertoire, and instead of dissecting the music to learn individual challenges one at a time, the students played from beginning to end, with little regard for process. This simplistic approach leaves gaps in learning where physical and mental skills need to be developed. Skimming over processes can hinder and even block students' later progress, if they encounter technical challenges that require the understanding of what came before. If students do break down learning and consider the various processes involved in a task, aligning these to subgoals, they can tailor and regulate their learning. The small goals and individual accomplishments can then be integrated into learning at appropriate stages during the overall task. For example, the specific requirements of physical coordination and the mental understanding of the thought processes involved in a task can be separated and dealt with individually instead of having the student attempt to attend to all aspects of a task at once, and when he or she is ready, all of the components can be brought together to successfully carry out that task.

Learning can be examined on a microscopic level by examining students' awareness of monitoring, methods, and beliefs that are involved in learning and relating these to their practical assignments. Relating individual learning experiences to the wider picture of a study or degree programme then gives students insight and allows them to draw conclusions about both how they can affect specific situations and the importance of their self-beliefs and self-regulation. Practically connecting concepts introduced in an academic context with assessment tasks and outcomes serves to interrelate theory and understanding, and makes the academic theory a real, meaningful experience.

...thinking about it

▶ What strategies or processes will you adopt while reading this chapter?
▶ Do you just read, or do you have a considered approach?
▶ Note this down *before* you read on, and then reflect on it after reading the chapter.

▶ Applying self-regulation

Zimmerman and Martinez-Pons (1990) set out ten different self-regulated learning behaviours (see below). The original context of the research was in a high school (secondary) academic setting, but these behaviours relate to any academic situation where people aspire to self-regulate their learning.

▶ Self-evaluation (judging progress during the task)
▶ Organising and transforming (rearranging material and/or the order it is approached; for example, learning might not start at the beginning, or the top of the page)
▶ Goal setting and planning (creating a hierarchy with timings and criteria)
▶ Seeking information (from non-social sources: published material, archives, recordings)
▶ Keeping records and monitoring (notes or recordings kept by the student)
▶ Environmental structuring (optimising the surroundings)
▶ Creating self-consequences (rewards or punishments)
▶ Rehearsing and memorising (going back over, consciously repeating sections or sub-sections)
▶ Seeking social assistance (working collaboratively, seeking advice or information from people – peers or teachers)
▶ Reviewing records (revisiting feedback or marks on past tasks)

These behaviours fall into the overall categories of planning, monitoring, and regulating (Garcia & Pintrich, 1994). As a practical example to demonstrate how these behaviours apply, consider the scenario of a student who has a project to complete as the final assessed course work that could be anything from a project that involves working with several media or a standard written essay.

▶ Goal setting and planning: The student might use the self-regulated learning behaviours listed above by creating a list of the components needed to complete the assignment and set an initial time scale for progress, creating a number of hierarchical subgoals.
▶ Seeking information – both from non-social and social sources: The student reads books and consults a tutor for guidance and to gain information.
▶ Environmental restructuring: Studying might take place in a dimly lit, noisy bedsit, or the student could choose to go to the library or meet at a friend's house to have a more quiet and comfortable working space.
▶ Keeping records, organising and transforming: The notes from collaborations with other students, research, and interviews can be read, rearranged, and put into a form that will contribute to the assignment.
▶ Creating self-consequences: These are rewards or punishments. Perhaps after a good evening of studying, the student might decide on a rewarding break for a film or a pizza.
▶ Self-evaluation, rehearsing and memorising: As the assignment takes shape, the student can assess how it is going, and perhaps revise it with another draft.
▶ Reviewing records, self-evaluation: Before completing the assignment, the student may look back on previous feedback to see if this project is an improvement on earlier work.

Depending on the task, using a particular behaviour may suddenly seem more obviously important, or one might be used more frequently than another depending on the context. It is surprising, though, how easy it is for both students and teachers to overlook some of these simple strategies for enhancing and optimising learning. When the assessment task is not integrated or related to the learning content of a course, then the subject curriculum and the assessment requirements may be quite separate and the taught content might not provide obvious opportunities to integrate and develop aspects of students' self-regulation as they prepare for their assessments. For example, if a course is taught as a traditional lecture about a historical period within the subject area (classicism, for example) and the students write a final essay, there could be little connection between listening to the lectures and the act of writing or preparing the essay, and thus the 'last minute essay' is possible because students are not required to *do* anything else beforehand. If there is not an inbuilt reason or opportunity for students to use self-regulated learning skills, and to apply them to the task at hand, some students will never entertain the possibility. One student recalled being in this situation: 'We weren't allowed to talk in lectures. We just sat there while some guy wrote on the board.' This is not an ideal learning situation, but it does happen. In this situation, the student with low self-efficacy will feel belittled and possibly give up. 'I got bored and stopped going.' The student with high self-efficacy will find a way forward. 'I ended up learning it for myself.' In a situation like this, self-regulation is essential for a student to successfully learn despite the situational challenges and lack of facilitation through teaching.

There is a definite need for educating students in strategic thinking. The percentages of students achieving the academic benchmark thresholds on the standardised ACT tests used in the US for entry into higher education were surprisingly low. Out of over 1.6 million students who took the test in 2011, the national percentages of those achieving the benchmark grade in the four core subjects tested were: English 66, mathematics 45, reading 52, science 30 (ACT, 2011). The ACT (2012) subsequently carried out a detailed study with 61 institutions offering four-year standard degrees. Students were profiled from their entrance test scores through to completion, and of the 125,911 students enrolled in courses, the percentage of students meeting benchmark standards in their entrance test scores, English 78, mathematics 38, reading 59, and science 26, followed the trends of the national study. These scores also were shown to have 64–71 percent accuracy when predicting the students' degree results. There was only a 42 percent completion rate for the enrolled students in the institutions represented, and this 'highlights the importance of students being ready for college and performing well academically in their first year to improve their chances of progressing towards completing a degree' (ACT, 2012, p.43).

In the UK, instead of requiring all students to complete the same components on a single standardised test, students elect both how many and which subjects they study at A-level, and these results are used when they apply to university level courses. Entry requirements usually require a specific array of grades, and to gain a place a student may need to meet a given level, usually within two or three specific subjects, requiring a suite of grades (such as: A, A, B or C, C, C) from the candidate's chosen subjects, which could be Physics, Chemistry, and Mathematics. Requirements will vary between subjects and from one institution to the next. In 2013, the Joint Council for Qualifications reported that 850,752 students in the UK took A-level exams across a range of 35 diverse subjects including law, religious studies, and Welsh (JCQ, 2013). Of these students, 77.2 per cent received a grade of C or above in their chosen subjects (JCQ, 2013). It makes sense that this number is slightly higher than the percentage of American students to reach benchmark thresholds, because the British students actively choose their specialisms and eliminate classes they do not wish to pursue. However, these percentages could still improve, and university entry remains highly competitive.

Higher education institutions commonly have established learning support programs with study skills sessions directed to specifically improve gaps in the way students learn and study for their course work and assessments. The principles of self-regulation and gaining access to instruction on how to apply these behaviours to learning are important for all students. Self-regulated learning is not a remedial or corrective measure. From the teacher's perspective, it is important to consider what strategic possibilities are presented to students and how they might incorporate self-regulated learning into their study habits and other work that contributes to their development. Hattie, Biggs, and Purdie (1996) suggest that teaching a single skill or strategy will give the most successful results, but within the higher education context this is certainly not the only method. There are mixed views as to whether self-regulated learning strategies are universal for all disciplines, and could be taught through a generic, supplemental or extra-curricular programme. The underlying skills and behaviours will transfer across contexts, and with slight adaptation they can be specifically optimised to best suit a specific subject area.

The University of Texas at Austin offers a modular class, 'Individual Learning Skills', which is taken for credit, as an elective class that meets over 15 weeks. It was designed around Weinstein, Husman, and Dierking's (2000) Model of Strategic Learning (MSL) and influenced by Zimmerman's (1998a) theory of self-regulation (see also Schunk & Usher, 2013). The MSL covers five core areas involving knowledge of (1) the self, current levels of skill and one's strengths and weaknesses, (2) the tasks, including criteria and the necessary or required skills, (3) strategies and skills, knowing what options are available to use, (4) content, understanding prior knowledge, and (5) learning contexts, relating to value and understanding how learning undertaken now can benefit future situations (Weinstein & Acee, 2013). In the class, students cover a number of topics that are divided up into shorter 2.5-hour modules covering specific areas of strategic thinking and learning. Each segment has an associated assignment to explicitly use the taught skills.

Higher education students, as opposed to younger school children, do have the capabilities of mature thinkers and are able to take on board complex concepts quickly (Wigfield, Eccles, & Pintrich, 1996). They are not without cognitive strategies and are generally very accomplished, having literacy and numeracy skills and not needing to be taught as complete beginners. By teaching a combination of strategies at once, alongside tactile teaching approaches such as modelling, students can gain an understanding of self-regulated learning behaviours as well as how to use them in practical contexts. The difficulty with students at the tertiary level is that they already have been in school for over a decade and have formed learning habits (Hoffer, Yu, & Pintrich, 1998), which can be difficult to change. Although higher education students are capable of observing and understanding self-regulation, it can be challenging to change their existing practices. Students who already achieve good grades may not see the need to alter what they already do, even if their methods are not particularly well thought out or efficient (Schunk & Zimmerman, 1998). Encouraging and embedding new self-regulation practices takes deliberate, and sometimes significant, effort.

An effective way to demonstrate to students the different impact is through their own achievement. For this to be effective the teacher guides the students through the steps towards achieving the task and avoids allowing the students to focus on any preconceived bias or prejudice about their capabilities to do the specific activity. This is a similar principle to the work Wegner, Schneider, Carter, and White (1987) did with the concept of the white bear (as mentioned in Chapter 3). The teacher needs to avoid a situation where students get in the way of their learning by deciding they can't do something, or need to unlearn something preconceived in order to progress. In terms of self-efficacy, having an unbiased approach to a new pursuit allows for the initial mastery experience to be achieved as a true 'first', and avoids the student erroneously perceiving low self-efficacy beliefs based on something they have not yet done. Unhelpful and incorrect beliefs are often because the student associates a new and daunting task with something that they have previously failed at or not approached well.

For example, if the student believes that they cannot spell or write a coherent argument, then sitting him or her down to write a polished, well-supported essay is not going to produce a successful result in terms of the work or the impact the experience has on perceived self-efficacy. When students have low self-efficacy beliefs, they are less likely to seek or use strategic thinking, and if they are not able to analyse, plan and set goals, then the magnitude of the task can be overwhelming. However, if a task is designed so they *do* succeed in achieving progressive goals, with inbuilt reflection and observation of the methods they use, then the experience can be used to positively reorient and rebuild their self-efficacy beliefs. When students directly achieve something themselves and are shown the paths they took to solve the problem worked, this can be the foundation for their own self-regulated learning.

As a practical example, I demonstrate this principle in workshops by intro-ducing instrumental playing as a new task. If presented with a violin or cello, some assumptions that a non-musician might make could include that this is not something for them, that only musicians can play instruments, or that it is very difficult, especially for an adult who is a beginner.

> **Case study 5.1: When staff become students**
>
> I returned to one university after working with their students to present staff with this new learning experience. In the morning before my con-ference workshop, 21 string instruments were set out on display, and I watched from nearby as people looked on with curiosity. A very senior academic within that university was there, saw the instruments, stopped, and asked me with interest, "Who's doing this? Are you playing these?"
>
> I replied, "Yes! I am playing, but (gently pointing to him, making eye contact, and smiling) *so are you!*"
>
> Without hesitation he emphatically said, **"NO I'm not. I CAN'T.** *I know* **I can't."**
>
> I smiled and encouraged him to hold that thought, come to the work-shop, and then see if he could still say that to me.
>
> This initial response of 'no' 'can't' was typical, and not at all dissimilar to how many students feel when faced with new tasks.
>
> It is so important that tasks are understood, approachable, and that the necessary strategies for success are presented and accessible.

These are examples of negative biases that need to be avoided if the first experience with the task is to be positive. Over the course of an hour, I talk people through the different physical and mental processes of holding the instrument, navigating the distances between the strings, understanding pitch relationships, and using the different parts of their body in new ways to hold the bow and depress the strings to make the notes. Because each task is individually simple, and can be compared to an everyday activity, the result is that the 'new' musicians are not afraid. They do not doubt that they can do the tasks because they are being taken incrementally through many subgoals. They are not yet aware of what they are accomplishing, but the component processes are presented in a way that they are achievable. After a certain point, when they are all playing a few notes, they are asked if they know what they have done and often someone realises that they are actually playing a tune, and usually shouts out, 'That was Twinkle, Twinkle!' If the task of even playing a simple nursery rhyme had been presented to the novice learners at the outset, it would have seemed impossible, but because they were already doing it, they could look back on a successful accomplishment. As a first mastery experience it is very effective: they cannot disclaim having played the song. They already have achieved it, and that makes any doubt about their capabilities unreasonable. The challenge is then to enable people to understand that learning process and to carry this forward, replicating it on their own, and to transfer it to other learning settings where they encounter something new. This will reinforce their self-beliefs about their capabilities for approaching learning, breaking down the concepts, and using self-regulation.

Metacognition and strategy use

There are various stages to using these behavioural strategies. A student first begins to understand the metacognitive knowledge, which Flavell (1985) describes as 'cognition about cognition' (p.104). When the processes are understood, the detail and choosing the most appropriate or relevant strategies can be processed, and finally this knowledge can be applied to the practical situation. Zimmerman and Martinez-Pons (1990) suggest educators use a triadic model of self-regulation as a tool for understanding the relationships of behaviours and how these can be contextualised within everyday functioning. In this model, the self-regulated learning behaviours are mapped onto the three categories in Bandura's (1986) model of functioning.

▶ **Personal processes** include organising and transforming information, rehearsing and memorising, and goal setting and planning.
▶ **Behavioural processes** encompass self-evaluation and self-consequating.
▶ **Environmental processes** relate to seeking information, keeping records and self-monitoring, environmental restructuring, reviewing records, and seeking social assistance.

Some aspects of self-regulation can occur as completely internal processes, without any external signs. For example, when a student thinks about what they are going to do, this can then be taken out of the category of unseen, personal processes and become an interactive, physical process. Likewise, planning and goal setting can be mental processes, and through verbalisation and discussion with others they cross over to become behavioural and mix with the environment through social interaction. After observing how high-achieving students adopted and used self-regulating learning strategies,

Zimmerman and Martinez-Pons (1990) suggested teachers use this model as a guide for instructing others in self-regulated learning practices so they could become more effective learners. Self-regulation can permeate all areas of everyday functioning, and an awareness of possibilities for how to use different methods is a starting point for teaching students to adopt these processes for themselves.

Ritchie and Kearney (in preparation) explored the impact of instruction on students' awareness and use of self-regulated learning strategies across various dimensions of learning. They had 20 volunteers from across a university population who were taught to play violin, viola, or cello over the course of a semester. Learning a musical instrument was a new experience for these adults, and as an experience outside their daily functioning it allowed a clear demonstration of when strategies were deliberately used in their learning. The 20 were divided into smaller groups for weekly music lessons. Half of the people had explicit instruction in how to learn and practice the material presented, with advice about particular self-regulated learning behaviours and strategies and how to apply these to the musical skills and repertoire they were learning. These people also keep a detailed diary in which they detailed the planning for every five-minute burst of practising, recorded when and what they practised, the methods used, and then reflected on the effectiveness of the session. The students without instruction in self-regulation were taught the same musical content in their weekly lessons, but they had no further explanation, demonstration, or advice on how to learn or what to do with the material in their own time, after they left the session. Instead of keeping a detailed diary of planning, methods, and reflections, this group was given a placebo task: they were asked to listen to some music of their choice and write how it made them feel. Everyone who participated in the study kept a minimal diary to record the dates and times they played their instruments between the formal lessons. Over the three-month course of lessons, all students had the end task of performing a selection of musical repertoire to the class and to a camera. They were allowed to choose one of the pieces, but there was also one required piece of music that students learned completely independently; it was never taught in class and this music was significantly more challenging than anything they were taught.

Some of the theoretical aspects of self-efficacy and self-regulated learning such as resilience and persistence (or lack thereof) were manifested in Ritchie and Kearney's study in very transparent ways. Interestingly, over half of the people who did not receive instruction in self-regulation dropped out of the study before the midway point, claiming frustration and saying: 'I just couldn't do it' and 'I wasn't making the progress'. All of the students who remained to the end of the study achieved a similar, basic level of performance standard, regardless of whether they had specific instruction in self-regulated learning. They could all play folk tunes that were clearly recognisable, and even showed some musical flair. The differences in how they arrived at that standard became clear when examining the practice logs. Those without instruction on how to self-regulate their learning spent twice as much time practising to achieve the same results as those who did self-regulate their learning. The methods used and the time they spent studying the music by those who did not use self-regulation were far less organised. Typically they 'played through' their music, whereas the group who had instruction on self-regulation attended to a specific detail in each session, used different approaches, and the methods presented in class were transferred into their independent learning time.

At the outset of the study these people were all competent adult learners and thinkers: some were final year students, others were department admin-istrators or student support workers. People volunteered from across the uni-versity. Regardless of their career experience and how efficient or good they were in their specialist area, they all needed direction to realise how to effec-tively apply learning strategies to this new challenge in music. It is possible to transfer self-regulated learning behaviours from one setting to another, but this may not be implicit or obvious to students. Just as self-efficacy can trans-fer from one situation to another if the criteria and underlying skills compare, students need to understand that the methods and behaviours associated with self-regulation can also apply to new situations. In order to be effective autonomous learners, students need to believe in themselves, cultivate skills, and understand how to use those skills in the different tasks and learning environments they encounter.

Self-regulation within the learning cycle

Self-regulated learning is 'an acquired capability composed of phase-specific processes that students apply repeatedly during learning experiences' (Zimmerman, 1998a, p.16), and the strategies and methods fit like Russian dolls into Zimmerman's (1989) three-phase learning cycle of forethought, action, and reflection. At the outset of the forethought stage, students have their own levels of intrinsic interest in topics and tasks, and they also have individual self-efficacy beliefs for learning and performing. Students' initial self-efficacy perceptions act as a starter for the whole process of learning and self-regulation, because when students assesses their capabilities and make judgements in their confidences, it informs how they proceed.

Depending on whether students have a high or low self-efficacy, they tend to exhibit corresponding traits of being either skilful or naïve learners

(Zimmerman, 1998b). High self-efficacy alone does not guarantee students will carry out tasks, as they also need to be motivated and value the outcome of the task in order to actually do it (Bandura, 1997; Wigfield, Tonks, & Eccles, 2004; Schunk & Mullen, 2012). Students with high self-efficacy tend to be intrinsically motivated and set mastery goals, with an interest in learning for the sake of improving their own knowledge rather than for an external reward or instant gratification.

Before the active learning begins, engaged students will apply their self-efficacy judgements, strategic thinking, and self-regulated learning behaviours to planning a series of subgoals to form a hierarchical system. Having goals allows students with high self-efficacy to self-monitor their progress as they can see the incremental steps they are taking (Zimmerman, Bandura, & Martinez-Pons, 1992; Zimmerman, 2000; Schunk & Pajares, 2009). Naïve learners set distant vague goals, and have an unfocused approach to their learning. Instead of being able to understand their learning, these students rely on feedback from others to be able to judge levels of achievement, and to monitor and reflect on their progress (McPherson & Renwick, 2001; McPherson & Zimmerman, 2002). Students practise self-instruction and seek information during the active phase of learning when attention is focused on details like coding and organising materials.

The self-evaluation that comes with reflection usually takes place after the active phase of learning; students can also pause during learning to make sense of progressive steps within a task. When a student has a structure of subgoals, miniature learning cycles are created and reflective pauses are built into an ongoing process of activity. This contributes to the larger context of learning, and when students reflect on their evaluative judgements, plans and goals for the next steps in learning can be appropriately assessed and, if necessary, realigned. Students with a strong sense of self-efficacy for their learning are more likely to accurately attribute progress to the strategies and behaviours they have used, whereas those who doubt themselves will less readily attribute their success to themselves, but instead to external circumstances or guidance from others (Zimmerman, 2011).

The students who lack self-efficacy and do not use self-regulation or strategic thinking to dissect and understand difficulties one by one, believe that willpower and brute force are required to overcome obstacles in their learning (Thoreson & Mahoney, 1974). Conversely, when those with high self-efficacy reflect on accomplishments, they own the experience and this makes them more likely to accurately reflect on their skill acquisition and use. In future assignments, those who have a strong sense of self-efficacy for learning will seek and develop methods they can control to improve on what they have already achieved. The way students perceive their circumstances, progress, and accomplishments affects their adaptability towards their future learning.

At key points within learning there may be rewards (or punishments) for the amount of progress made, and when reflecting on these, students make important attributions about their accomplishments. When students have to undertake a required task such as an exam, where they have no choice in the activity and the final grade is received after the learning process has finished, the effects of that task, the grade, and the feedback received on self-efficacy for learning, self-regulation, and motivation can be marginalised (Schunk & Ertmer, 2000; Schunk & Pajares, 2009). Without choice, the active role of the self is removed and self-regulation involves the student in a continual and active cycle of monitoring, evaluating, reflecting, and planning. If this is all prearranged or done for the student by the teacher, then the task is no more than following along a dot-to-dot type path, and when the student completes the task he or she will have neither the experience nor the understanding to sustain the activity on his or her own.

▶ Reinforcing self-efficacy beliefs

There are many mechanisms that can be used to enable and reinforce awareness of successful learning, to aid students in moving from relying and being guided by external influences to being internally motivated and responsible for their own learning. As students accomplish tasks and begin to integrate taught strategies into their learning, they also build their self-efficacy beliefs, but this is not an automatic process. The awareness gained from self-observation reflections on learning and progress can be used to formulate self-efficacy beliefs, but students need to be aware of processes and feel ownership for their actions and achievements. For some students this seems natural, while others struggle and cling to the security and reassurance of teacher's strict guidelines and instructions. As self-regulation develops, the clarity of reflections, observations, and acknowledgement of successful experiences confirm positive self-efficacy beliefs. These positive beliefs feed into the learning cycle, perpetuating a loop that leads forward to meaningful choices and reinforces students' self-efficacy for learning and performing beliefs.

Becoming self-sufficient

It is not enough to be taught to think strategically or to have a grand repertoire of skills; students need to actively take control, prepare, shape, enact, and monitor their learning. When students make the move from being aware of and using strategic thinking under guidance to doing this on their own, then they begin to self-regulate their learning. Being self-regulated and having ownership of learning does not mean that there is no longer a need for input from others. A teacher's advice and instruction is invaluable, and can complement the thought and engagement of the student.

Being responsible for choosing and guiding learning requires an outlook that distinguishes between short- and long-term goals and processes. Zimmerman and Martinez-Pons (1986) categorised the self-regulated learning strategies into six dimensions (see below, left).

These groupings are intuitive and parallel basic modes of questioning: Who? What? When? Why? Where? How? These dimensions align neatly with aspects of a learning experience that can be regulated by the student.

- ▶ Motive   Why?
- ▶ Methods   How?
- ▶ Time   When?
- ▶ Outcomes   What?
- ▶ Physical environment   Where?
- ▶ Social environment   Who?

Within each of these dimensions, there can be any number of self-regulated learning strategies and behaviours, personal attributes, and self-beliefs that are appropriate and useful for different learning situations. Questioning and breaking tasks down sectionalises and structures the learning process from the beginning and can be another tool for students to use when considering their assignments or project work and beginning to make sense of how and what they need to do. Simply having a list of strategies without a framework for their application can be daunting and even detrimental, as not all will be able to see both the detailed- and grand-scale picture of how to work step-by-step and towards the whole goal. These dimensions provide a framework that can help combine and apply what the student knows about themselves, their self-efficacy for the task and for learning, and their repertoire of strategies.

Scaffolding

Scaffolding enables students to create their own opportunities to build self-efficacy beliefs (Schunk & Usher, 2012). Forming a hierarchy of goals first requires seeing an endpoint. This is not necessarily a final goal, because, for some students a final goal may be too distant. With a large piece of coursework like a dissertation or research study, going from the initial planning to completion is too much to represent in a single goal, as there will be many iterative steps to the learning process and there can be considerable unanticipated change along the way.

For a student, having a vision that connects the immediacy of what is at his or her fingertips to the fully formed, final assignment is very important and can be crucial for being able to take the step from being a strategic learner who is good at following instructions, to becoming a self-regulator. Professor Hans Jensen described the relevance of this process for musicians.

> It's important to have a vision, an internal understanding of what you want to create. The more you can give a vision to a person, inside their own head about what they have to do, the better they can do it. You can't do anything you can't visualise, and it's unlimited what the mind can visualise. If you aren't completely clear what it is going to be in the end, if you don't have that ability to really have discipline in your practice and to control your mind, then it is going to show up. ... The strength to succeed and really show what you want to do starts in practice. (Jensen, 2013)

Jensen speaks of a musical setting, but this relates to both the student and the teacher across disciplines. For experienced learners, they will be more equipped to structure their visions into practical and attainable sections, but for a less confident learner there may be a need for more guidance. In either case, the teacher needs to have the foresight and holistic understanding of the whole of the task and its processes, so that if and when the student needs reassurance, it can be provided.

Teaching students to plan and have a core goal requires them to understand criteria, look ahead to plan for the next step in learning, evaluate and re-evaluate what they need to do in light of what they have just accomplished, and to continue to stay focused throughout learning, until the performance or completion of the task. This is complex to teach and takes patience. No one teacher could be expected to take responsibility for this, especially if the student does not have a history of methodical, strategic, independent working.

Focus and concentration are actually most realistically maintained when accomplishing a sequence of small goals instead of having one distant goal. Less experienced students often simply repeat the same processes without giving a thought to monitoring or evaluation (McPherson & Renwick, 2001). These students repeat their habits without awareness of the hindrance they cause to learning without making or achieving specific goals. For students it can be a revelation that it is acceptable and even productive to work incrementally and have breaks in between individual steps or subgoals. With breaks, it is much easier to focus the mind, giving time to refresh the mind, reflect, and reassess the situation. A positive effective process will reflect on the student's perceived self-efficacy beliefs. With guidance, students can be productive with cycles of as little as 20 seconds of deliberate concentration on a given task, followed by a pause to evaluate the effectiveness of what they have done before moving on to either repeat or revise their next strategy. Jensen challenges his students to see what they can accomplish by spending one minute a day on a new task. One minute every day equals a half hour a month, and six hours a year. When students' attention is brought to processes on a detailed level, it can illustrate how and why they can benefit from choosing to adopt certain behaviours.

When students do recognise the steps they are taking and structure incremental steps into their learning, then teachers can be affirmative by highlighting progress and periodically guiding students through tasks.

> Yes, you have completed xxx, and how will you begin the next phase of your work?
> Having established the underlying principles gives you a foundation for your experiment/research/writing.

The teacher acts as an external reminder to confirm when benchmarks or standards are met, and acknowledge accomplishments. When feedback is trusted and reliable, it is a form of verbal persuasion that will influence and reinforce self-efficacy beliefs.

▶ **Understanding progression**

Ertmer, Newby, and MacDougall (1996) stress that the teacher needs to be aware of the student outlook and of the reaction to instruction, and this will facilitate the appropriate level of encouragement and support. Those students who do not understand how (or why) to self-regulate may be unfocused, vague, or even fearful when confronted with a new task (Schunk & Usher, 2011). *'It's difficult. I don't know where to start.'* Others will avoid challenges through procrastination. With awareness, teachers can support and direct students to realise and understand what they already know and show them how to bridge the gaps that lead to new learning.

Case study 5.2: How students understand and apply modelled behaviour

In a study of learning methods and self-regulations, first-year veterinary students in a biochemistry laboratory course were introduced to new learning concepts through a series of specific cases (Ertmer et al., 1996). The researchers theorised that this experience would give opportunities for students to self-regulate their learning, becuase placing value and importance on what is taught and on learning outcomes has been shown to have a positive relationship to students' levels of self-efficacy, engagement, and motivation (Schunk & Usher, 2012; Schunk & Mullen, 2012). The students who were considered higher self-regulated learners did value the instructional models and saw their direct application to wider learning. These students set specific criteria-based goals and used strategies that allowed them to analyse and effectively self-regulate their learning. The students who did not already have high levels of self-regulation had a 'limiting' attitude towards the instructional model (Ertmer et al., 1996, p.735). Instead of choosing appropriate strategies, or creating new ways of approaching the learning, monitoring progress, or adapting their approach, the students who displayed less self-regulation tended not to plan for their work. These students followed old habits, even when these were not effective or appropriate for the current learning context.

Understanding progression requires students to accurately assess what they have done against what they expected. In primary school learning, teachers do this for students when they regularly examine pupils' work through worksheets, reading diaries, small quizzes, or tests. In higher education, a continuous cycle of feedback from the teacher to monitor progress seldom exists, and in many large classes it would be impossible. Less-experienced learners desire this safety of being told what to do and how to do it, because this removes the requirement for them to self-regulate their learning and think independently.

Progression within the context of a degree may be clear from one module or year to the next, but this can be less obvious if individual classes are self-contained and sit outside this framework. In many institutional programmes there is a strong aspect of chronology and order, with prerequisite skills and knowledge that link from one level to the next. Seeing progression across various classes requires students to implement elements of self-regulation. As students compare their current skill levels to where they were at the outset of learning, they begin self-assessing and interpolating wider meaning from their progress.

Planning safety nets

When students face a new task, they need both criteria and goals in order to monitor and reflect upon their work. When an assignment only has a single end goal – an essay, presentation, or a performed task – that may be the student's only opportunity to outwardly demonstrate their learning. Having some level of initial confidence is valuable, especially for those who tend to be weaker students. If they are not confident, they may delay as long as possible to avoid exposure and facing a potential failure, whereas if they are confident then they will more readily seek opportunities to test what they know and succeed. A teacher's support can encourage students towards that first step of choosing to independently seek and apply strategies to their learning. Once students begin the process of learning, they overcome the perceived barriers of what they do not know and begin to see the value of how they can use their skills. With time and experience they can move towards experimenting and feeling comfortable with becoming more active, reflective, and generally facilitative towards their learning. Throughout the stages of learning, students can benefit from various frameworks where teachers bridge the gap between, by providing avenues for assistance and time for reflection, so that when challenges arise, students can adapt and self-correct the course of their learning.

In the context of music performance in my own institution, when students prepare for a formally assessed music recital they are encouraged to give several complete public performances before their assessment date. Students are provided with lists of performance venues, but deciding to make contact and arrange a performance is up to them. The choice is left to the student, and although this activity is suggested to guide and encourage them in developing self-regulated learning behaviours, the mechanism is not a fail-safe because it is optional, and there are some students who choose not to perform externally. On-campus performance sessions are timetabled into the curriculum and act as a safety net to guide all students towards actively rehearsing the exam situation and self-regulating their learning. These do prepare students for the assessment context, but these sessions are in an informal setting and cannot replicate the true sense of a real public performance. Occasionally there are weaker students who still attempt to shy away from engaging even with these informal sessions. If students have lower self-efficacy for learning and for performing, they will have a more vague, unfocused outlook, and can avoid looking for help as it could expose their weakness (Zimmerman, 2011). More efficacious students engage with scheduled sessions and also take the initiative to arrange their own performances, and the experience they gain has a markedly positive impact on their confidence when approaching the final assessment.

Students who are given complete choice over their learning sometimes skip important steps that require basic repetition to embed, and this can 'undermine the emergence of forms of long term motivation' (Zimmerman, 2011, p.60). Many students need mechanisms for support that are readily available and integrated into the curriculum them to access as needed.

This can be facilitated through allowing time in or after seminars for peer reflection or discussion on progress, providing templates for self-reflection journals or course blogs, or other forms of peer feedback via forums or online focus groups. Structuring goals for students' time and accomplishments can be a useful exercise. For example, with an essay, by week 2 topics and abstracts are drafted and shared with peers; by week 4 outlines and a minimum framework for research is complete; by week 8 half of the essay is drafted and the remaining half of the essay exists as a detailed outline; by week 10 a full draft can be shared for peer review; and finally in week 14 the final version is submitted. This is a very loose example, and can be translated to any type of project, where a weekly reflection on progress could be shared, or videos of work in progress. The teacher can suggest a few key points to guide student planning. Without being exact or prescriptive, but by giving a framework for evaluation and reflection, the students have the flexibility to reshape their work and make the learning and their progress their own.

Assessment in progress

Receiving feedback encourages reflection and promotes strategic thinking, but having work assessed by a teacher is different from self-assessment. Formally assessing student work is usually the responsibility of the teaching team, and along with grades, students receive comments about their work. Courses have scheduled points when students are required to engage with assessment, whether mid-term exams or other formative tasks whereby feedback is gained to develop understanding or help students prepare for future assessments. Students may read comments, internalise some of the advice, and reflect on how it impacts their current level of accomplishment and what they need to do to improve. Having times when students reflect on their work structured into a course can provide an opportunity for students to revise a working pattern and choose different strategies as they proceed towards completing their assignments.

Without a required, structured task and clear criteria, many students do not know how to begin to assess their own progress and simply skip the important process of questioning how they are progressing. Self-assessment implies that this is something done by the individual, and if it is not included as an in-class activity, there may be no outwardly visible signs for the teacher to know whether students are self-assessing as they progress through learning. If students begin working incorrectly and do not assess their progress they could be set up for failure and not realise this until after the final grade comes back. Identifying errors, troubleshooting, and having the opportunity to make improvements are very valuable before the final work is submitted. Having semi-structured points where students can judge themselves against benchmarks or criteria can enable the student to self-assess. When students are aware of accomplishments and these are positively reinforced through reflection on feedback from assessment and self-assessment, this can motivate students and strengthen their belief that they can strive further.

▶ Exploring and experimenting with creativity

Within teaching and learning in higher education, patterns do arise and students become accustomed to typical ways of learning. When a class steps outside of those expectations, it provides the teacher with an opportunity to refresh and revisit students' perspectives on their learning processes and capabilities. The two examples in this section change student orientation and responsibility to their learning, creating a situation that calls for students to have confidence, apply self-regulation, and reflect.

Case study: #Phonar

Jonathan Worth's undergraduate #*phonar* class at Coventry University was designed specifically to leverage the Internet as a resource for both the teacher and a learner. It was launched in 2009 and has grown to have over 40,000 students attend classes in a single term (Hartmann, 2012). The numbers are accommodated because besides being a credit-bearing class for students enrolled at the university, it is also accessible to anyone for free via the Internet. The course is structured with various tasks and subtasks so students outside the university can dip into the content as and when they want to. There is a strong element of choice, and when a student does take on a task, the objectives and criteria are clear. Weekly taught sessions that take place at the university with enrolled students are broadcast for the larger learning community, and students develop bonds and draw support from one another. Through the weeks, students post their work online through various social media and blog websites and tag it with #*phonar* so staff and fellow students can locate submissions, view, and comment on each other's work.

Students are encouraged to have their own ideas, and, as the teacher, Worth provides carefully chosen examples that simultaneously inspire and spark students to have their own thoughts. There are some students who weave themselves into the fabric of the class by actively providing feedback to peers, and they enter what Worth describes as a sort of 'social contract' where they respect and value opinions. Students develop independence through giving and receiving support and comments, and this acts as feedback to inform and confirm students' judgements about their learning and work.

Putting work forward for a widespread public display, such as the Internet offers, adds another layer on to the processes of learning and draws upon new confidences within the student. The act of posting necessitates that students are aware of their work at that moment and they have begun to assess even in a small way to make the judgement that they want to post it. This is different to submitting work solely to receive teacher's comments, and is also different to only self-assessing a work in progress. The students' judgement that their work is ready to post may be made against criteria relating to the assessment, or simply against their personal standards. The personal standard might be considerably higher or lower than the task requires, and it then becomes a useful tool for transitioning students into their professional practice, where often they must set their own standards for work. There is a community created through this worldwide sharing, which allows students to be active models throughout the course, by posting coursework and notes across various platforms (with tweets, photos, and videos). The nature of the online systems allows students to monitor who has seen their material, to leave comments and read comments by other members, and to witness how their participation has a wider impact beyond their fellow learners to the wider learning audience across the Internet.

Teaching the teacher

Part of my teaching includes actively learning from my students. This is not a trendy way of saying that teachers learn via the experience of teaching, which does happen, but learning from students in this context is a separate, genuine undertaking, as opposed to a planned lecture, demonstration, or modelled situation. Reversing the roles of the teacher and student can go beyond modelling and putting students in the same situations as the teacher, where they can assume responsibility for strategising. This can demonstrate the practical application of self-regulation and the transfer of beliefs and strategies from one setting to another. It allows students to explore their understanding of learning approaches through something that is live, communal, and removed from simply applying self-regulation to an independently assigned task.

Within music, there is scope for many different and related activities that share common elements of experience and learning theory across the various instrumental specialisms. For example, different instrumentalists can teach the same musical concepts: a French horn player and a viola player can both teach the understanding of phrase structure, although neither may be able to play the other's instrument. Teaching performance techniques on a given instrument, however, is quite separate and requires different knowledge and skill from teaching concepts that are common to all instruments. My students study how to teach, and how to communicate, and in instances when their teacher (me) becomes the student, the realities of student progress, mental and physical weaknesses in learning, achievements, and the complicated mix of non-musical factors that come together to impact learning can be brought to life in a very real way. They are able to sit outside of the learning processes they engage with every day and see them afresh.

The teacher-as-student experience works in various situations. Students can observe and critique the teacher in a professional role. The students were invited to take on the role of the teacher and assess my performance when I appeared in a concert as a soloist with the university orchestra. They engaged with the performance aspect of their learning journey, by using assessment criteria and providing a mark and comments as feedback in the same way as they would experience at the end of the semester. Reversing the roles of teacher and student suddenly changes perspectives, and the largest gain was that the processes of learning and achievement were demonstrated with a dramatic reality. Students could see the connection with criteria, and they in turn were able to dispel unwarranted anxiety about what had previously not been understood with the assessment process.

Teachers becoming students can take place any time there is a specific skill set and interpersonal communication takes place. As long as there is an unscripted interaction that unfolds as in real life, then the student can gain a genuinely beneficial experience as they engage with metacognition to analyse, plan, strategise, and act on the situation. Issues of interface and communication become tangible, and students experience and apply learned concepts about self-regulation in an active way. It is a completely different experience and perspective to listening to a lecture or reading a text.

A teacher may have excellent specialist knowledge, but it is inconceivable for every teacher to have specialist knowledge in all areas, and this leaves room for learning, and for improvement. Teachers can also genuinely take on the role of being a student. As a musician, I specialise in the cello. When I am a voice student, as described in detail in Chapter 7, I have technical aspects of singing that need to be learned: understood, internalised, practised, and reproduced in an effective and fluent manner. For the student (me) this takes dedication and the development of skill, and requires the teacher to communicate and observe and adapt to the changing needs of the learner. Both when the students observe another learning and when they take on the role of teacher, it facilitates a fresh understanding of roles. Sometimes students overlook their own learning, and it can be easier to recognise processes in someone else and then relate that to their own experience and reflect on how they carry out their academic learning. As a student, all of the typical thought processes, challenges, doubts, and learning achievements can be presented and discussed. The university students take my teaching more seriously when they realise that I am not just teaching them theoretically or telling them what to do, but am also willing to put myself through the same learning experiences that they are required to undertake.

There is no limit to what students can be shown when they are in the learning space with the teacher, but the introduction of skills is not enough in itself to sustain self-regulation (Zimmerman, 2011). Students need the understanding, access, and motivation to use these skills on their own time. This cannot be an additional burden on the teacher, and with too much teacher involvement the independence and choice are removed. It would be naïve to expect the teacher to check the implementation of self-regulation at every step, but through careful use of behaviours and strategies, students can use self-observation to assess their progress and seek help as needed. The instruction received from teacher mentorship and modelled situations can create a culture where 'responsible interdependence through guided learning propels accountability, perseverance, and motivation' (Mullen, 2011, p.141). Engaged learners draw upon their self-efficacy for learning to sustain their motivation as they work towards completing goals (Schunk & Mullen, 2012).

When students have an active choice in their learning, they begin to successfully manage their learning and take steps towards independence from the classroom (Zimmerman & Bandura, 1994; Zimmerman, 2000), and this can be confirmed through external resources, such as tutorials or feedback, to support and confirm progress. Schunk and Usher (2011, p.290) discuss the positive impact on self-efficacy that identifying and transferring skills from one situation to another can have on learning and approaching a new task. When transferability is recognised, it can dissipate some of the fear that comes with approaching new assignments.

Further resources

▶ For examples beyond the arts and a step-by-step guide on how to bring self-regulation into the classroom, see Barry J. Zimmerman's (1996) book *Developing self-regulated learners: Beyond achievement to self-efficacy (psychology in the classroom)*. Although written for middle and high school settings, the book provides clear scenarios with principles that underpin learning and can transfer to settings in higher education.

▶ The *Peeragogy handbook* (available from http://peeragogy.org/) is also an excellent resource that provides examples and case studies of co-learning between students and teachers in different educational settings.

6 Self-efficacy in practice: Outcomes and attainments

The relationship of self-efficacy beliefs to goal setting and achieving outcomes is explored in this chapter. The value of attainment is considered in how interim stages of learning activity can act as positive preparatory experience for final assessments, forming foundations for positive self-efficacy beliefs, and marking progress towards successfully reaching goals. Instances where teachers can help students to choose, plan, and organise learning and experience are discussed. Finally, links between the qualities developed through self-efficacy and self-regulated learning are related to professional practice and entering the workforce.

Realistic planning and specific knowledge of skills and approaches is needed to successfully accomplish tasks and ensure that students have positive experiences to build their self-efficacy beliefs for future engagement. It is often challenging for students to develop a clear vision of their final, or end, learning goal and how the details of daily activity fit into the overall concept of arriving at that goal in a productive and effective way. To maintain self-efficacy and maximise the efficiency of learning, students need criteria, parameters, a sense of timescale, and a concrete measure of accountability. The process of planning and accomplishing subgoals will eventually become routine for the student, but as when encountering any new material or skill set, these processes need to be introduced and learned.

Creating opportunities for students to articulate goals and subgoals through different means, in and out of class time, enables them to take responsibility and gain a sense of ownership throughout the learning process as they progressively achieve their goals. The development of analytical and perception skills gives students a broader contextual understanding of their learning and progress. When working at this micro level, the student becomes quite aware of the intricacies of skills and processes, and begins to create and reinforce good goal setting habits that can be recreated in various future settings.

The accountability that comes with delivering and producing outcomes develops learners for the professional setting. The initial reason students choose to pursue a task may be simply to pass an exam, to please themselves or impress the lecturer, to prove a point to peers, or genuinely to learn, but overall goals are more complex and include a multifaceted web of factors. Students must balance these to find a focus that is both enticing and sustaining enough to drive them to complete the task. The importance of various factors may shift as students progress through their studies. Self-reliance and self-regulation are excellent skills, but once learned, they need real-world applications. Having frameworks, methods, and routines built in throughout learning allows students to be prepared, having considered both the task-specific elements and environmental pressures that come with the professional settings.

▶ Developing and fulfilling goals

Throughout the higher education system, students encounter various models of assessment, ranging from a single examination point at the end of the degree, to exams at the end of semesters or modules, to classes where final marks are aggregates of several elements of coursework. There has been a noticeable move from the traditional essay/exam to expand and include a range of portfolio work, presentations, and written components (Sambell, McDowell, & Brown, 1997). There is an art to learning to manage assessments in the context of learning, and each task will have differing levels of familiarity to the students, explicit structure or guidelines, criteria, and importance within their programme of study.

The element of choice and personal agency is important to students so they can have ownership of their work and learning, but at the same time there is still a need for guidelines both to enable students to achieve relevant outcomes and to help teach them how to create their own parameters when they continue learning outside of the educational context. Overly prescriptive assignments provide regimented goals, but the ownership, drive, and, ultimately, the impact on self-efficacy is limited because students seldom see achievements that they are forced into as something that truly came from them. For example, the standard essay question can fall into this category of assignment. From the student perspective, they have been taught through years of school examinations and expectations that if they study they will be able to achieve the 'right' answers, in reproducing facts to demonstrate understanding, and this cultural outlook can lead to a narrow view of personal possibilities. Thus students' perception of their personal agency, expression, and learning potential in completing an assigned goal can be very low. As educators it is possible to see many ways of creating an activity or assignment that is as in-depth and inventive on a defined or required topic, and many great thinkers found freedom in having rules imposed for them.

The composer Stravinsky, who pushed many boundaries in music such as in his controversial *Rite of Spring* said:

> Well, in art as in everything else, one can build only upon a resisting foundation: whatever constantly gives way to pressure, constantly renders movement impossible. My freedom consists in moving about within the narrow frame that I have assigned myself for each one of my undertakings. (Stravinsky, 1970, p.65)

For Stravinsky, the rules that surrounded him were the very things that enabled his expression. The assessment type, the criteria, and guidance that go with it can be either limiting or freeing for the student. It is amazing how a small change in wording or presentation can completely alter a student's perspective on what is being expected and of his or her possibilities with that assignment. For example, in a few of my classes students are required to write a traditional essay that is submitted at the end of a term. The assignments come with relevant criteria on aspects of the written style, from the formatting to referencing to having a coherent content, and criteria about the inclusion of relevant musicological and critical quotation. What is missing from the criteria is anything requiring a specific topic. Some students relish this freedom and it inspires and motivates them, and for others it is paralysing: '*I don't know what to do if you don't tell me.*'

Learning to approach goals is a task in itself, and especially if this is new or seems new because it is different to what students have done in the past, they may not be confident about doing it. More distant assessments can present other challenges to students' understanding of their progress towards a final goal. Conceptualising and formulating the path of learning requires a sense of structure and hierarchy. Students need not only to have goals, but also need to be able to create their own interim goals and subgoals to continue to develop their learning and maintain momentum throughout their studies.

Self-efficacy and decisions

Students have more than one type of self-efficacy belief relating to their assessments. They will have specific self-efficacy beliefs for each aspect of a task, and on the microscopic level they will have beliefs about their capabilities for the overall performance task in the end and for the processes along the way. Both self-efficacy beliefs for learning and performing are informed by how students understand what is being asked of them, understanding where they are now, and the skills they need to develop. These beliefs are intertwined with aspects of motivation and external factors to impact the practical choices students make about approaching their assignments. Personal motivation, the timescale involved, and the scope of the assignment's importance within a grading scheme for that class and within the student's overall degree will also influence the student's decision making.

As students are faced with coursework, they plan, choose, and organise various courses of action that propel them towards achieving their goals. Depending on the task, students will experience very different levels of motivation and of confidence in their current level of ability and in their perceived capabilities to navigate the processes involved. Self-efficacy for learning is relevant at the beginning of the process. The students' understanding of what is required for the task and of their own grasp of useful skills for learning heavily influences their self-efficacy beliefs and whether or not they accurately project a path for their learning and work.

Students who delay starting their work on an assignment if it is due at the end of the term may do this as a conscious decision, as opposed to procrastinating, but for students with lower self-efficacy, who may also be weaker academically, there can be a strong element of avoidance (Zimmerman, Bandura, & Martinez-Pons, 1992). Students do not like to fail at the end or at any point in learning. If there is uncertainty about the level of skills needed for that task, then avoidance means that students do not have to expose and reinforce their weaknesses. Planning for learning has to do with perceptions of capabilities, an awareness of the component skills required for learning, and of how to access information and build components towards a goal. The way students engage with an assessment is a direct reflection on their self-efficacy for learning and performing that task. Self-efficacy for performing beliefs also inform engagement and career choice (Bandura, Barbaranelli, Caprara, & Pastorelli, 2001); if a student is very unsure of the task, then he or she will avoid it. A student who has strong self-efficacy beliefs will make different decisions about how to approach the task, what to do to proceed, and how to deal with times when he or she is faced with doing or integrating skills that are new to them.

These planned choices point back to how well students are able to self-regulate their learning, as emerging autonomous learners, and all of these components come together in how they are able to put the pieces together towards a final assignment. Specifically in courses where there are large student numbers, the taught content can be very different from the mode of delivery of the assessment. There is a difference between how good a student is at the subject or how good he or she is at delivering a convincing essay about specific facts within the subject area. Writing an intricate essay on the character development in post-Renaissance opera does not mean that the person is a good tenor, violinist, or conductor. Initial self-efficacy beliefs can be shaped and influenced so that the student has the best possible outlook towards coursework. That initial fear of completing a new task can be alleviated by gaining experience of similar, related tasks.

Assignments as rehearsed assessments

In higher education, students are aware that studying any subject will require work, especially to explore the content in depth, and there are also parallel expectations by teachers that students will be asked to demonstrate their understanding of what has been taught. However, there is a chasm between the technical understanding and the practical application in a real-world setting that cannot necessarily be captured through written words alone. Sometimes students are required to produce a summative essay, and other courses may require a portfolio or a presentation as the vehicle for assessment. Still other courses may be working towards a more practical goal where students demonstrate understanding of the mechanics of a deliverable service or task, or are in a position to engage with others in the professional world. Where real-world applications may not be practical to assess with a big cohort, an essay may be an efficient use of the teacher's time. Hybrid models that include practical experience and require reflections in academically produced writing allow students to prepare and compare.

When students do have assignments that seem distant, being due months in the future, it can be difficult for them to create goals and actualise the steps necessary to achieve to their potential in terms of performance and to experience the deepest learning possible during their time with that subject matter. To encourage a structured approach and address the underlying learning concepts, the final assessment, or aspects of it, can be replicated in a series of more proximal assignments. Using the template of the final assessment to create similar assignments as interim tasks may not be seen practical by the students. If students are required to write an essay or script and shoot a film as their final submission, requiring several other essays or films may be seen by the students as too much work, or even as irrelevant, especially if these are not weighted towards the assessed grade.

As part of the undergraduate degree programmes at the University of Chichester some students write a dissertation essay that ranges from 7,000 to 12,000 words as their final assessment. In the UK this is a common part of degrees and typically stretches across the final year of the degree. Many students see this dissertation as both a distant and weighty goal. There may be additional weighting for the dissertation element of a degree programme; for example, sometimes gaining a distinction in the degree result also depends on receiving a distinction in the dissertation element. Essays are not uncommon in modular or semester-long classes, and even when the endpoint for the assessment in sight, it can still be daunting and difficult for students to organise their time and learning towards that end-goal.

In order to encourage students, facilitate experience in specific tasks, and to aid with the practicalities of structuring time and progress, my own music students are required to write a substantial 7000 word final essay and are asked to produce between 500 and 1000 words on related topics every week. This writing is not formally graded, but is integrated into the class through peer assessment and discussion. Students have an element of choice to tailor the subjects to be directly relevant to their individual research topics, giving the smaller weekly writing tasks meaning and relevance within the overall structure of the final assessment. It is possible that students weave several of these smaller essays into their final submission, thus motivating students to complete these without the need for formal grades. Students' time management is indirectly influenced, and the smaller tasks help students to compartmentalise their workload and accomplish their work progressively throughout the course of the semester.

There are settings where the assessment task diverges from the practical skill base that the student is developing for a professional career, such as with a music course that requires essays. In this case, another way learners can develop confidence and prepare for the final assessment is through progressive tasks that reinforce the underlying learning that they are asked to demonstrate in the essay. This usefully builds the student's self-efficacy by gaining familiarity in a meaningful way with the concepts they need to articulate. If students know how to carry out the task, but are not fluent or confident with the subject matter, there can still be avoidance even of asking for help, so as not to expose them to potential failure (Bensimon, 2007).

Gaining familiarity with aspects of the assignments and learning the requisite skills to accomplish that final goal is likely to produce a more favourable outlook towards the assessment and achieving the tasks. Struyven, Dochy, and Janssens (2008) demonstrated this with a range of assessment types from multiple-choice exams to aural exams to portfolio work. Students regarded unfamiliar assessment types with negative attitudes and uncertainty. Developing practical experience with those assessment types not only changed the students' preference for that mode of assessment, but also their opinion of its appropriateness for assessing their learning. As with any initiative, there will still be students who choose not to engage, despite the accessibility, usefulness, and practical nature of interim tasks presented. Making the relevance of interim tasks clear to students enables those who are motivated to achieve to take advantage of various mechanisms presented to them within their learning environment.

Affirmation through feedback and reflection

Having completed smaller related tasks in advance of the final assessment, there is time for students to adapt and reflect on their work before having to assimilate it into the final submission. They gain the experience of having practised the skills required in the final assessment throughout their learning. Adding several interim tasks can only be sustainable in a teaching context when it does not impact the workload of the teacher. Accomplishing tasks does not necessitate that the student has reflected, understood, or attributed the experience as something they have personally achieved, all of which are necessary for both completing the learning cycle and for developing self-efficacy beliefs. Incorporating feedback encourages student engagement and in turn success in their education (Tinto & Pusser, 2006). Providing a range of perspectives, experiences, and modes of articulation and evaluation that students can relate to and absorb, on different levels, facilitates communication and helps students gain an understanding of the processes involved throughout learning.

Asking students to read each other's writing or view projects and provide criteria-based feedback as routine develops the skills of explaining and expressing a judgement on what has been presented and communicating how it meets the chosen criteria or not. A reflective exercise such as this provides layers of benefits. When students provide feedback to one another, they have a social reason to complete the task, even if the work does not contribute to the final grade – so as not let each other down. They actively engage with criteria to consider whether their peer's work attends to these, and formulating feedback to others can require tact. Examining the work of others is a form of modelling that becomes useful experience as students turn to look at the progress and quality of their own work. It may be that after several iterations of either individuals providing feedback or group feedback discussions, that students are then asked to provide feedback where they self-critique their own work and perhaps eventually present this.

Gardner Campbell uses the medium of blogs extensively as a tool in his teaching and says:

> *Any* conversation about what one is learning will tend to reinforce one's commitment to that task. One's learning is reinforced even through sharing questions and uncertainties. ... Blogs are hydroponic farms for heuristics, hypothesis-generation, metacognition that continually moves out to other metacognizers and back to one's own reflection. (Campbell, 2008)

Reinforcing the learning and developing self-efficacy beliefs through teacher comments can be an important step in this process. Peer mechanisms may accomplish the full circle of learning for some students, but there may be others who are still in need of that extra level of reinforcement, whether from their own uncertainty or from a lack of understanding of the processes. This can be achieved through semi-public feedback either in blog settings or through virtual learning environments online or in physical classrooms where groups discuss, and there is an awareness of, the feedback being received and digested instead of being delivered on paper alone and perhaps never read.

In settings where the class size is very large, teachers can use a randomiser to create small groups of students to work together. Large classes may be prohibitive of having small group discussions or plenary sessions on highly individualised interaction, and in these cases a teacher can still use this strategy, so that individuals can compare their work and feedback to an exemplar, which could be either a teacher-devised piece of work or another student work. The work used as the example does not have to be the most exceptional, but does need to demonstrate a clear relationship between the work produced, the criteria, and the feedback. To continue the discussion and ensure that students understand how they have progressed and can improve, a further layer of feedback can be provided by peers as to how that particular piece can be improved. At the beginning of this process, a teacher-crafted example can be of any level, and either separately commented on or put into the mix to be peer-assessed. This way, no individual is exposed as either being exceptional or working below a standard level, and students can readily see relationships and the value of the exercise. Peer learning and reflection can be encouraged when collaborative, problem-based learning is used to create a 'pedagogy of engagement' (Tinto & Pusser, 2006). When students engage with each other and with staff in learning, they have a greater likelihood of persistence and of success in their pursuits.

▶ Actualising success in formally assessed settings

Students can approach assessment with a strong sense of self-efficacy when the sequence of events and experiences leading to that point have been recognised as meaningful contributions towards their learning and performing. A formal assessment represents a staging post, the culmination of the learning experience for the duration of that class. It provides a fixed point for students to demonstrate achievement and then to check their beliefs against their actualised successes. Some students find formal assessments stressful for many reasons. A fear of being assessed can be perfectly justified if the student has not learned the material and, naturally, does not want to face that. In that situation, it would be incorrect and detrimental for the teacher to attempt to bolster the student's self-efficacy if he or she does not in fact have the skills. When students do have the skills, they still sometimes exhibit doubt. The complicated mechanism of the relationship between the teacher, motivation, and the social arena can either hinder or enhance student attitudes to learning and achievement (Urdan & Schoenfelder, 2006). Especially if the task is less familiar to the student, the teacher can be influential and supportive by affirming the student's skill, and this can give the student the permission needed to acknowledge and own his or her self-efficacy beliefs.

A formal or final assessment will differ from preliminary tasks that are more like dress-rehearsal experiences. It can be difficult to realistically anticipate a formal or final experience and replicate the pressures and expectations that will accompany it. Teachers work to prepare students for the experience of assessment by incrementally incorporating various possible scenarios and aspects of the assessment so that, under pressure, the student is prepared to accurately demonstrate their capabilities. Sometimes the gravitas of a 'real' assessment can throw a student if they have not been practising their performance along the way.

Incremental tasks should build familiarity and experience with various aspects of the subject and skills associated with carrying out the specific assessment, to foster and support self-efficacy beliefs for completing that task. Not every assessment is an essay. Especially for presentations and other tasks delivered in real time, tasks that lead up to the assessment should be developed or chosen to highlight skills and to familiarise students with the external factors surrounding and involved with the assessed situation, such as time limits, the physical layout of the venue, and the physicality of delivery.

...thinking about it

When you prepare to give a paper or presentation, do you consider the preparation as rehearsal for the actual event?

► Do you practise performing?
► Do you expect students to prepare for what they do, and do they know how?

'Performing' through assessment

Students spend years learning, compared with days of being formally assessed; when this imbalance in experience is redressed, teachers will find changes in the pattern of students' attitudes towards different types of assessments and the outcomes they achieve (Struyven, Dochy, & Janssens, 2008). This does not suggest that the stressful pressures of yet more exams should be imposed across the weeks of study. Completely the opposite: assessment is a judgement point, and this can be filled with the positive celebration of achievement just as it can be loaded with negative associations. When the process of assessment is understood and students are prepared, they can regard it as a check that reflects and confirms their attainment. Students who are prepared and confident in all aspects of a task and its assessment will not be held back from achieving by doubting their capabilities. Students with accurate, stable self-efficacy beliefs do not necessarily achieve top marks, but their self-beliefs will not impede them in achieving to their full capabilities. However, if the skill is there and the belief is not, then students will not be able to achieve to their full potential (Collins, 1982; Ritchie & Williamon, 2012).

Students learn to assess, just as they learn to study. When gathering this experience, it must be separated from learning because the skill set used is different and much more aligned with performing (Schunk & Pajares, 2002). Students are carrying out the execution of a task in assessment, much like a performance where they apply the skills and knowledge that they have already learned and rehearsed. An examination is not the place to consciously work on acquiring new skills. Still, there is learning in the act of being examined through whatever means, and students gain the skill of delivery in that mode of assessment, but in the moments of delivery they draw upon their existing, prepared knowledge. Encouraging students to understand the differences between learning and performing can enable them to move forward in their work more quickly. When students shift their viewpoint and reflect on these differences, the understanding of what new skills are used in performance comes to light. In music the idea of 'performance' is very obvious, as a violinist may stand in front of an audience and play music by Bach, and this situation is understood as a performance. However, *learning* to perform in music is no less difficult than in any other discipline. Even though in music, performing is a related outcome of the learning, students still have to be taught how to perform. This involves creating mock situations and learning the skills to treat these as if they were the final moment of assessment. Being able to do this without the formality of the lights and the stage is a challenge.

Students across disciplines can put themselves in a position where they practise a set task, whether that is an assessment or performance, before it happens. This could be in the space of the final event, in a classroom, at home where the student studies, or even within the space of their mind. There are elements of thought processes that occur during a learning situation when a student questions and reflects on what is happening that hinder a performance or the delivery of a task. When performing it is not the time to doubt or decide to experiment with new, unexplored methods. Teachers can encourage an awareness of the difference between how students study and learn skills and how they perform a task. Understanding this and applying it in a practical context is valuable.

The value of tasks

Self-efficacy is a key personal, evaluative belief that influences choices and impacts attainments (see Bandura, 1997; Zimmerman, 2000), but it is not the sole force driving people's decisions. People need motivation to take action, and in order to succeed they also need skill. Assuming that students have acquired sufficient skill to succeed, they are often very motivated to choose, learn, and carry out their chosen tasks. However, students are not always inherently motivated to do tasks that are unequivocally required of them as part of their studies. Sometimes the larger educational framework can dictate students' route within a prescribed programme of study and then students find themselves jumping through hoops instead of leading their learning. Where elements of choice exist, students are more likely to have some form of personal motivation associated with their choices, and this will lead to a feeling of having personal agency, and of ascribing meaning to that task. Eccles and Wigfield (2002) define value as 'attributing personal significance or importance to an object or activity'.

Having choice empowers people, and even when students believe they have enacted a choice, these decisions are often made with inadequate or incomplete information (Eccles, 2005). There is a need for familiarity with the task to make accurate self-efficacy beliefs (see Chapter 2) and of the processes involved so students can effectively evaluate and assess their learning progresses (see Chapter 5). Specifically in academic settings, students find themselves in the position of not being familiar with the format of the required assessment tasks (Struyven, Dochy, & Janssens, 2008), and having the necessary experience, detail, and clarity to make accurate judgements is essential to establish and build self-efficacy. Even though people do make choices based on what they think is necessary, having accuracy makes the processes and progress that much more efficient.

In settings where students have few options to choose their specific classes, they will still value the functionality of their chosen specialisation or major

(Wigfield, Tonks, & Eccles, 2004). Elements of choice can be presented within very structured courses that allow students to make informed decisions and give students a sense of freedom and ownership. Students might develop aspects of exam questions, choose topics, choose between different formats for their assessment, or devise their own independent projects. Choice does not need to appear in every aspect of the students' experience for them to find meaning and value in what they do. When a teacher creates a practically relevant focus for required tasks, then these experiences can be turned from situations that students might otherwise avoid into engaging and valuable parts of their learning.

Tasks gain attributed meaning from a mingling of a student's perceptions, expectations, and self-efficacy beliefs for learning and performing that will lead to the achievement of the task. If students perceive an assignment to be useless and not what they want to do or have chosen, then motivation will be low, and even if a student has an adequate sense of self-efficacy for that task, it will not be perceived as having an inherent, intrinsic value. Thus, any learning accomplishment will have little impact on developing self-efficacy beliefs and the student may even choose not to engage with the task (Wigfield & Eccles, 1992). Meaning can be ascribed to the task if the student's perspective is shifted to see the importance of process or skill, giving it a practical, utility value (Eccles, 2005). The teacher can highlight the relevance of the underlying concepts learned and show how these can transfer to other settings or goals that the student has chosen to pursue or wants to achieve in the future.

Timperley and Phillips (2003) demonstrated this shift in belief and engagement when delivering professional development to teachers with a model that included new specialist knowledge that gave a deeper understanding of why the task was useful, an awareness of self-efficacy beliefs, and actively monitoring and recognising aspects or elements of progressive achievements. These worked together to produce a sequence of positive changes in both student and teacher behaviour. The combination of belief and engagement becomes useful and integral to the hierarchy of learning, and the student is far more likely to undertake tasks with a sense of purpose and value. As a result, there will be more likelihood that this positively will be reflected in their self-efficacy beliefs for that task.

Values require accountability. The personal significance associated with value implies a relevance to something lasting that becomes a part of that person's developing sense of self. The understanding and association that goes with a statement like '*I am becoming a writer*' has a more widely substantial and relevant enduring quality than '*I got a B for my English composition.*' If a sense of value is established within assigned tasks, this will infuse into the student's other pursuits. When students value individual processes for how these contribute towards their continuing learning development, this sense of value will transfer beyond the individual academic experiences and eventually become integrated into their professional lives. Values are set apart from goals in that they are ongoing, whereas a goal can be transitory. When students complete a task and reach goals, they can move on and leave that experience behind when progressing to the next challenge. Finding the centrally valued qualities within an assigned task establishes and facilitates a reciprocal loop between acquiring a sense of value, the purpose of the task, and the reinforcement of the accomplishments that result from gaining them.

Core qualities like resilience and perseverance that are associated with self-efficacy are valued across disciplines and can be made context-specific within any discipline. There will be specific qualities or skills that are perhaps technically oriented that will be valued and admired within individual specialisms. Tasks can have different values that are beneficial to the student's sense of self-efficacy. For example, when someone enjoys a task as they carry it out, it has intrinsic value (Wigfield & Eccles, 1992), and this can immediately influence motivation and feedback as a positive experience of learning to reinforce self-efficacy beliefs. Considering a task for its future usefulness in the overall scheme of learning towards career development is more of an extrinsic value, as opposed to something where someone experiences immediate, personal value. Embedding both intrinsic and extrinsic value into exploratory coursework, assignments, and assessments can have a great impact on student outlook and commitment towards carrying out their tasks.

Dr David Preston (2013) made the connection between personal agency and value when describing how 'watching what happens when learners have permission, [it] gives them a sense of value', when speaking in his TEDx talk about how his class was able to take personal responsibility for leading their learning and making it their own. In Preston's teaching approach, he allows the learning experience to move beyond traditional classroom lectures and assignments, to become a game that extends the thinking into other areas of that student's life. The idea of being in control during your turn in the game is natural, and helps to dispel any lingering tendencies the student may have to be a passive recipient instead of an active participant in his or her learning. Elements of the teaching methods used to transform learning in his English Literature class (see Preston, 2014) can be applied across disciplines. Students direct their learning, and this necessitates a sense of self-efficacy to successfully approach, understand, and carry out the tasks.

The value of achievements

Achievements can be bridges that connect a student's starting point to his or her future learning and career goals by building on values and principles developed throughout learning and the skill acquisition process. Achieving a result marks an arrival, and how that is valued can influence students' ongoing goals. Both extrinsic, achievement goals and self-efficacy influence the outcomes of students' tasks (Plante, O'Keefe, & Théorêt, 2013). When achievements have meaning that students internalise, they are more likely to draw upon their accomplishments and relate the achievement and associated value to new pursuits, approaching these with a stronger sense of self-efficacy.

Students can follow or aspire to what they perceive to be valued either by teachers or some abstract institutional or professional framework that may not exist (Eccles, 2005); for example, students may choose a contextual history class not because they want to study that topic, but because they think they *should* because they think that topic holds some secret significance or value within their study or employment prospects. The wider framework of a course, and how various tasks are relevant, can be clarified and reinforced through teacher advice. Bringing the focus back to the individual's development will dispel any effort by the student to create or attribute a false meaning where there is really nothing but presumption or rumour. When achievements are viewed in terms of an individual student's acquisition of mastery and not as a ranking system or means of social competition, then the value of an achievement is in its contribution to the portfolio of the student's developing professional skill base and that individual's persona.

People are drawn to tasks that align with their personal sense of value (Eccles, 2005). Students may not initially see how the results they achieve could relate to the wider context of their professional future, because it can be a challenge to look ahead while in the midst of study. Bong (2001) found students' self-efficacy beliefs became more aligned with both the intrinsic value and the understanding of how tasks could be useful for future learning and achievement in cases when students had received mid-term feedback on their progress from the teacher. The teacher's guidance reinforced students' positive beliefs in their developing achievement and guided their attention to areas that could be improved. Giving detail about their achievements and the tasks through feedback is an important part of the developing framework and relationship of self-efficacy beliefs and achievement values.

Developing self-efficacy is a collaborative effort that draws upon many elements of experience and perception, and it relies on the internalisation of experience. In Boud, Koegh, and Walker's book *Reflection: Turning experience into learning*, Heron (1985) discusses the challenges of reflecting on learning and taking forward the essence of what is learned to new situations (p.131). Working to reduce the social comparisons and increase students' personal knowledge and awareness is a starting point. Teachers can then facilitate and carry this awareness and reflection throughout learning and follow it through so students can pinpoint and articulate aspects of what they can take from their accomplishments and in turn relate and apply their learning to their beliefs.

There is power in learning skills, as opposed to facts, for individual contexts. When students begin to infer meaning from class experiences and assessed work, and can transfer learning from their current situation to other contexts, then their achievement and success has a lasting value. Associating the successful assignment as something that has meaning moves beyond achievements being grades with letters or numbers. The resulting grades students receive are external labels given to achievements to represent what has been learned, but the task process and the development that it has given to the student is what has lasting value.

▶ Careers and impacts

The self-efficacy component of social cognitive theory does more than identify a contributory factor to career development. The theory provides the means for enhancing the personal source of control over the course of one's self-development (Bandura, 1997). The findings of the current study suggest that children's career trajectories are getting crystallized rather early in the developmental process. ... Modeling supplemented with guided mastery experiences provides an especially effective vehicle for building resilient self-efficacy. (Bandura et al., 2001 p.202)

To some extent students in higher education are guessing at what tasks will be most beneficial to their future careers, because when they begin their studies few students have practical experience or a comprehensive understanding of the complete skill set necessary for a professional setting (Eccles, 2005). The specific impact of students' choices on their future success, from learning individual skills to choosing whole courses, cannot ever be certain, and without understanding or even having adequate information, anticipating the future can seem an even more impossible task to the student. The teacher's word is a powerful persuasive tool that can reassure and guide the students, especially as they build and formulate their career paths. Nowadays employability involves more elastic qualities as well as concrete skills, and embedding practical experience alongside the more abstract values that come with developing self-efficacy and self-regulation into a degree programme helps to prepare students for their transition to the working world (Bridgstock, 2009).

Professional security through skill and belief

Definitions of employability have expanded across the world from a traditional view that having developed requisite skills or knowledge makes someone employable to also include an array of wider qualities (Bridgstock, 2009; CES, 2009), from organisational and management skills to self-beliefs. Employability now encompasses a broad spectrum, and the importance of qualities that focus on the self and applications of skill (Pegg, Waldock, Hendy-Isaac, & Lawton 2012) is demonstrated in the four main points presented by Knight and York (2004) with the USEM model of employability:

► Understanding
► Skills
► Efficacy beliefs
► Metacognition

The USEM model reframes knowledge as understanding, recognising an element of deeper learning. Metacognitive processes underpin many aspects of strategic and self-regulated behaviour, and without efficacy beliefs these would not be combined into an effective employee performance.

   Students who embody these qualities, and are therefore seen as readily employable, reach a point where they begin to self-complete the learning cycles of Kolb (1984) and Zimmerman (1989, 2002). When faced with a situation they are able to explore and dissect a hierarchy of possibilities and make creative and informed decisions that balance risk and effectiveness in their actions. Having established the practice of good learning habits and reinforced these through evaluation and monitoring gives students an advantage ahead of fellow graduates who have not yet made the transition from the safety of the classroom. UK Quality Assurance Agency for Higher Education has specifically published guidance focused towards developing employability of students that stresses the need to build self-efficacy and to develop personal skills and attributes that support independent ideas and ownership of actions (QAA, 2012). Pool and Sewell (2007) introduced a model of employability that clearly included self-efficacy as a key factor that linked from the subject-based knowledge that they termed the CareerEDGE

(Career knowledge, Experience, Degree knowledge, Generic knowledge, and Emotional intelligence) to employability.

Tschannen-Moran and McMaster (2009) explored ways of practically building self-efficacy through dedicated professional development for teachers, from the design of different strategies through to using these so the teachers see impacts in the application of their teaching. A structure of achievements that were supported by mechanisms of further training effectively developed positive self-efficacy beliefs. The training programmes to develop the beliefs and practices of these teachers parallel the positive learning experiences of students in higher education. The study reinforced the practical need for support, and the teachers who had positive experiences combined with additional learning to reinforce their own accomplishments showed the largest increase in self-efficacy beliefs. Development of these beliefs is not something that happened with textbook knowledge alone, nor was it shown to be as effective with an isolated and unsupported instance of task mastery, but it required all of the influences of self-efficacy to be present and to be reinforced over time.

Beginning with self-efficacy

It is never too early for learning to focus on mastery, from the initial stages of awareness, through the approach and methodology, to the resulting achievement. Studies with young learners have shown self-efficacy to predict career choice (Turner & Lapan, 2002) even more strongly than academic achievement (Bandura et al., 2001). The beginning stages of learning are influential in shaping decisions, and although this is stressed with students at the beginning of their education, there are parallels with students in higher education. The level of specialisation in the particular areas they have chosen for their careers is often new, and these students are exploring new skills and their applications for the first time. Their decisions to follow certain paths will set a sequence of events in motion that determine which skills are developed and could either open or close doors leading to future experiences.

> If institutions are serious about developing graduate attributes or employability (with their implications for interaction between students), then the challenges posed by assessment have to be addressed. (Yorke, 2010, p.10)

Each opportunity and how it is received feeds into the cumulative experience of the student. Every assessment brings the student closer to the completion of their degree and entry into the workforce. For the curriculum to best prepare students, it needs to link the practical scenario to and through the methods of assessment wherever possible. Enactive experience that lets students demonstrate their skills moves beyond learning *about* the subject to creating experiences with the subject. In vocational courses it is commonplace to have workplace or placement experience. Consider learning to drive a car: in the US drivers are required to complete a set number of study hours in a classroom, observed driving hours that are often a combination of time in a simulator and on the road, and hours gaining experience on the roads (DMV, 2014). When studying for a teaching qualification, this is required. It makes sense that wherever possible students gain experience of the tasks that they will carry out so they are able to approach the profession with established confidence in their capabilities.

Taking it to the streets

The practical tools that students are equipped with by learning about a subject are of little practical use if the students are not secure and confident in their beliefs about using them in wider settings. Applying skills learned through coursework in practical situations can involve more than the initial demonstration within the stable structure of an educational environment.

Within music studies, students have a variety of performance assessments that are treated as any other timetabled exam. Depending on the institution, these assessments may not be open to the public. Sometimes only final recitals are open to the public, and students sit closed-panel type assessments during other interim points in their degrees. The transition from the institutional lecture theatre to the external concert hall is more of a step for students than it might seem, even within the performing arts. The musical content of these assessments might translate directly into a public concert setting, but if specific technical material such as scales is assessed, then this is not likely to be suitable for a general audience. For the student to make the transition to the real-world context can take encouragement, self-direction, and, certainly, self-efficacy, not only for performance but also for managing the new situation and dealing with the unexpected. Even in a discipline where it seems that it should be natural, only the proactive and visionary students seek their own opportunities to link learned skills beyond the assessment structure while they are still students.

A strong sense of self-efficacy can work to remove perceived barriers to career entry and progression because people can confidently adapt and persevere in the face of challenges (Lent, Brown, & Hackett, 2000). The physical environment impacts and interacts with the student's sense of self-efficacy as it is tested in practical situations. Self-efficacy will be either reinforced or challenged as the student evaluates new situational factors and uses strategies to adapt and navigate real situations. Facing these challenges with a secure, strong sense of self-efficacy can be achieved if there is a history of accomplishment that includes a portfolio of situations that deal with factors that students will encounter within the professional setting. Teachers can plan a graduated approach that transitions from the classroom to the workplace environment, guiding students towards successful encounters involving more or different variables.

> Positive experiences with change, embodied in the sense of mastery, accomplishment, and professional growth define the success of the change and its continuation in practice. (Struyven, Dochy, & Janssens, 2008, p.70)

This shift from the classroom to the workplace needs to be embedded throughout the experience of higher education, and not just in vocational courses. The practical elements in such courses are attractive and essential parts of the provision, and there is a push in current educational thinking to make the pedagogical principles of applied learning a part of any curriculum (Gibb & Haskins, 2014). Students learning more traditional subjects are not without direct applications to employment or professional settings, and some of the established approaches and methods found in education and artisan courses could be borrowed and adapted for these settings. The values, the personal qualities, and the repeated practice of experience all contribute to building self-efficacy beliefs that are secure and become woven into that person's everyday working methods and habits.

7 Implications for life-long connections with learning and teaching

Establishing a strong sense of self-efficacy sets the foundation for a continuing pattern of learning and achievement that happens through professional development and an active pursuit of personal growth. Planning, seeking, reflecting on opportunities for training, and peer co-learning can facilitate a positive career trajectory and keep a teacher's perspective fresh and fitting with today's fast-changing workplace. This chapter considers the ongoing development of self-efficacy as someone moves from being a student to having a professional career, and challenges teachers to reflect and strive for continued life-long learning.

There is a moment during each graduation ceremony, as students have completed their studies and walk to receive their awards, when they symbolically join the academic community represented by their teachers who sit on the stage and applaud their achievement. In practice, however, there is no magical epiphany of rebirth and these graduates are much the same as they were the day before, when they were still students. Having confidence and self-efficacy beliefs for what they do and developing experiences that enable these people to join a professional community is something that begins in education and continues to build over years. The formal graduation does release that learner into the world and cuts some of the ties with the institutionalised structure that has set tasks and parameters, reinforced learning, and provided an external, recognised framework of validation in the form of teacher feedback and grades. Anyone can access learning networks once out of education, but once a student leaves the nurturing setting of higher education this requires motivation, resilience, self-reliance, and a firm sense of self-belief both to seek and pursue both communities and mechanisms of support.

Self-efficacy forms a foundation for future experiences. The beliefs that have been built over the years of study are the residue of the experiences, and for each person, they are like potter's clay that has been sculpted into the shape of confidence and a sense of security in what he or she can do. Having a solid grounding in their self-efficacy equips people with the skills to analyse, attribute, plan, achieve, and grow throughout their lives.

▶ Professional development

The need for continued learning and development for all people is recognised in higher education, starting with the central mission of teaching students and through to developing the teachers' own skills and up through developing the layers of management. Students are being prepared to practice life-long reflection through portfolios that develop throughout their time in higher education. Many institutions require students' engagement with reflective electronic portfolios that accompany and supplement the regular learning and coursework (Tzeng & Cheng, 2012; Abdullah, Ward, Catterall, Hill, & Wilson, 2013). For some this serves as an experience log and bank of information to use when building personal statements for future jobs, or creating a curriculum vitae. Having a record of achievement and reflection on experience serves to reinforce self-efficacy beliefs and strengthens the link between the education world and the professional marketplace.

Teacher self-efficacy beliefs are important so that training and development programmes can be effective and have a direct impact on teaching practices and student learning (Lumpe, Vaughn, Henderson, & Bishop, 2014). For teachers, professional development has come to be expected, and it ranges from standardised instructional sessions to explaining new educational tools, software packages, or how to follow newly adopted institutional procedures, to more personalised sessions aimed at developing specific skill sets like communication or even enhancing well-being. Across diverse disciplines, professional development is associated with 'updating' or the 'acquisition' of knowledge, and traditionally continuing professional development programmes address developing the skills needed to function and understand the systems used in the workplace, improving IT training, and keeping current in the field. Standard staff development courses cover using an intranet or a learning management system, managing Excel files, how to apply for a grant, how to be an effective manager, mental health awareness – the list could go on. These are traditional, information-based topics that are often taught with a didactic approach to development (Webster-Wright, 2010), essentially teaching the professional in the same way a student would have been taught 30 years ago, as a receptacle for information.

Annual checks on teachers' engagement with personal development can take place through observations to demonstrate their use of learning, or in meetings with managers to discuss and document performance and progress against previously agreed targets. A Professional Development Plan (PDP) is a common tool used in professional settings where both practical skills and the developmental needs of the teacher are analysed and addressed through a series of targeted action points, which can either be pursued as self-directed or supported activities, through sessions organised by the institution (Daunert & Price, 2014). Formal meetings where a PDP is set or reviewed provide a place to document goals, achievements, and how teachers plan to grow over the coming year, and they act as a concrete record and reassurance of quality among professionals. Scheduled meetings and documentation can be seen as a chore to simply scrutinise productivity over the past year in a formalised box-ticking exercise. However, articulating accomplishments and goals gives people an opportunity to reflect on their learning and to project future developments that are fundamental and essential to their development as professionals. The process parallels what is asked of students, and reflection, goal setting, and recognising achievement are all powerful learning tools. Externalising these and outlining targets highlights capability and will affirm self-efficacy beliefs. Teachers can use an e-portfolio to reflect, and such portfolios can provide a mechanism to create a learning community where teachers can gain peer support and share aspects of their individual learning journeys (Ehiyazaryan, 2012). New learning and reflection leads to growth and development; it can contribute to a practitioner's currency in the field, and acts as fertile ground for new ideas and practices in teaching and communicating with students.

External influences

Continuing Professional Development (CPD) courses often take someone outside the daily workspace and place him or her in the setting of being a student again. Entering into a setting where the professional takes on the student role in a student–teacher dynamic has a host of implications for the way the professional teacher learns and how he or she views the experience. When teachers become content with their existing teaching style they can resist change or development, and engaging meaningfully with professional development requires a positive mixture of factors including the teachers' personal attitudes and beliefs, the type or context of the development activity, and how these interact in the everyday professional setting (Smith, Hofer, Gillespie, Solomon, & Rowe, 2006).

There are abundant training and professional development programmes for teachers in primary and secondary school (Blank, De las Alas, & Smith, 2008), but in the context of higher education, teachers often seek out means of developing skills and undertaking further training suited to their specific needs. When this is via an external course, held outside the normal work setting, concepts may be introduced through activities or workshops and may be very creative and helpful to the way someone can advance or improve their working. However, upon returning to the office or classroom, very often it is difficult to replicate the situation and implement change (Smith et al., 2006), and the day-to-day application of the concepts into existing routines of work can pose practical and personal challenges. This is not because of a lack of skills understanding on the teacher's part, but due to a combination of practical factors and the interaction of motivation and self-efficacy beliefs. In a training course, whether held in a physical meeting space or on the Internet as a MOOC (massive open online course) with discussion forums, each setting creates a separate learning space and its own community. Few training activities are thoroughly integrated into daily teaching activities, as this would require an instructor to have an intimate working knowledge of each participant's unique teaching situation, resulting in a bespoke scenario. This would be a luxury and an asset to any development programme, but it would require considerable time and financial investment to develop and deliver.

After a training course there are pressures of making up for lost time and continuing to meet existing expectations of students and colleagues, and this can make changes or additions to an existing routine daunting and make teachers feel pressurised (Webster-Wright, 2010). Adopting a new approach can feel like a personal risk, because if it fails and colleagues or students can notice, then this can feel exposing and reflect back on the teacher as a lack of capabilities. It requires a strong sense of self-efficacy to be able to take in the new learning, assess the current situation, and find ways of implementing the enhancements that have been learned. When things do not go well, in the same way as the students do, teachers need to be able to correctly attribute the cause of the situation, and this will allow them to maintain a sense of self-efficacy, as long as they know the preparation and all within their control was attended to. The 'daunting doubt' that inhibits people embracing change is a cloud that hangs over many people. In order to dispel uncertainties, teachers need the same mechanisms for support and for building positive mastery experiences and self-beliefs that are provided for students. When management use resources to help minimise negative influences in teaching situations and openly allow teachers' to innovate and take risks, this creates a culture of growth where teacher's self-efficacy beliefs will be strengthened and new ideas can develop and flourish (Tschannen-Moran, & Hoy, 2007). Having a supportive working and teaching environment with an invitation from management, encouragement, and a culture of engaging with continued learning and taking risks cannot be underestimated.

Beginning with self-efficacy provides a foundation of confidence to examine a situation, unpacking the different factors and processes to relate and apply newly learned principles or skills to a teaching situation. For example, upon returning from a course on developing connections that 'asks learners to experiment, to be active, and to be hands on, to be entrepreneurial in their learning, recognising that this is what is needed to be successful in work and life' (Connected Learning Alliance, 2014a), a teacher's enthusiasm alone is not enough to enact change. The teacher needs to hone in on the new ideas and craft a way to integrate these in practice by using critical thinking, progressive goal setting, and a plan to sequentially implement aspects of the new concepts. The self-efficacious person will be resilient, and this is important when bringing ideas into a new context. This process needs to be scaffolded, combining the approaches of Vygotsky (1978) and constructivism (Jonassen, 2013), both of which draw upon aspects common to self-regulation with seeking solutions, finding strategies, and verbalising thought processes. As moments of reflection are integrated into the process, the awareness of progress is realised and the constant check and realignment of goals becomes embedded into everyday activities.

▶ Learning to teach while teaching to learn

Formal individual training and mentorship programmes designed to personally develop the teaching practices of experienced individuals are not always offered through established development programmes. Institutions recognise the need to induct new staff, but ongoing development of teaching at higher levels can be left to the individual. As educators, each teacher needs to nurture and develop personal goals and set timelines for accomplishments both in and out of the classroom. As a measure of quality teachers are routinely observed by managers or other senior members of staff, who may well have relinquished much of their teaching roles. When this happens, judgements or guidance given based on the observed session may be fed back from someone who is essentially no longer an active teaching practitioner in that field. Tschannen-Moran and Hoy (2007) found that neither novice nor experienced teachers based their self-efficacy beliefs on the feedback from administrator evaluations. When observation is actively encouraged and carried out by peers, this can create a new learning dynamic that encourages an exchange of ideas and generates the development of practices within a given subject area. However, a direct openness is not commonplace in academic settings, and instead there tends to be an insular approach to teaching that is partly dictated by heavy demands on time from teaching and research commitments.

Yes, the experienced observations of senior staff are both invaluable and necessary for overall quality procedures, but the views of managers, heads of department, and deans are not the only views to consider. When teaching and striving to improve teaching and learning, it makes sense that there is also a consideration of the impact and opinion of those being taught. What if, as a complete change from established protocol, teachers learned from students? These are the people with the most current experience of learning, and they are in a position to provide regular, incremental feedback as regular teaching sessions unfold across a term or semester.

In the setting of co-learning there is a mingling of the student and teacher perspective. Students are learning to teach themselves while they learn to learn, and the teacher is receptive to the interaction in a way that is not possible with a traditionally predetermined didactic curriculum. In co-learning, the agency is given back to the student, and as a preparation for life, this is a valuable skill.

There are significant differences between school learning and the goals, methods, and expectations of learning within higher education. With a rather terse description, Illeris (2007) asserted, 'school socialises children to accept the performance of externally determined activities according to the bell' (p.219). This is vastly different from the environment in higher education that fosters students as individual thinkers who work as partners with educators to develop the values of trust, community, responsibility, empowerment, and authenticity (HEA, 2014, p.4). Students have to learn with the job as they change from the school setting to that first experience where autonomous thought is encouraged and expected, and it takes many of them by surprise that the teacher is not there to do it for them (Stephenson, 2012).

Engaging with specific tasks within the field, alongside the added responsibility that comes with learning in higher education, allows students to personally find validity and a reason for their tasks. As a result, the mastery they achieve has meaning and develops their self-efficacy. Gibbs (2014) posits that students can 'promote the idea of student action and agency through their online work, much more so than in the passive sit-and-listen mode of most classrooms' because the Internet makes student actions visible. Carefully structured teaching and learning in any environment can act as a positive dress rehearsal for life where students are already putting conceptual learning into practice through doing, and each action they accomplish within their studies affirms and builds their self-beliefs.

Learning with the job

There is a recognised need in higher education for teachers to learn and understand the 'scholarship of teaching' by actively pursuing this through professional development (Nicholls, 2001, p.110). Learning to be a teacher in higher education, to develop creative, skilled, autonomous professionals, is not often taught as a methodology within subject specialisms or in traditional programmes. For example, do engineering, physics, or even art majors learn to teach other students their specialist knowledge or skills? When people find themselves in a teaching position at a university, many essential teaching skills are often developed through experimentation of trial and error in situ, with real students. As a stark contrast, those studying to be school teachers do have rigorous training and education teaching them about learning and development, and they gain practical teaching experience before setting foot into a classroom unattended. In Germany, Belgium, France, and Japan, student-teachers are required to undergo extended university training and have weeks of mentored service as they learn by working in local schools before they teach their own classes (Darling-Hammond, 2008).

Observed teaching sessions, annotated plans, and having a mentor are effective ways of developing teachers' self-efficacy beliefs and completing the cycle of planning, learning, and reflection. A mentor provides a sounding post for ideas and plans, and can validate and encourage through feedback. Often in education, new employees have a mentor, but this is a practice that is beneficial to all levels of teachers, as communication can serve to externalise and reinforce thought processes. The impact of mentoring and the specialised continuing development of self-efficacy beliefs were demonstrated in a study of 125 workers employed in various municipality divisions. These people were relatively new employees embarking on their careers, and after being mentored they demonstrated both higher performance and higher self-efficacy (Day & Allen, 2004). Having a mentor requires the mentee to allow for the fact that there is more he or she can learn, and not all teachers are willing to admit this, especially once a position of authority within the academic culture has been reached. Exposing someone to new learning makes the possibility of vulnerability and failure real, but with this openness also comes the opportunity for growth, and without taking the risk to learn there can be no progress.

Some development activities or courses are delivered on the home ground of a teacher's own institution. For example, a Postgraduate Certificate in Learning and Teaching is offered in many institutions in the UK, and it is encouraged that academic staff, especially newer members, participate in this programme to develop their teaching skills. When courses have reflective elements that integrate directly into everyday teaching situations as part of the coursework, learning is embedded into activity. This keeps the teacher engaged while teaching instead of creating a separate learning environment, and this facilitates a smooth transition into, potentially, lasting change. If there is a cohort on a course, then a sense of community allows for peer interaction, observation, feedback, and the teacher's own contributions, which all work to build self-efficacy through three of Bandura's (1986) main influences: mastery, vicarious experiences, and verbal persuasion.

Furthering professional or academic qualifications, or outputs that provide tangible, auditable outcomes such as certificates, research papers, and the development of subject-specific skills via a certified course are also valued by employers as PD activities, but learning and developing teaching skills are less foregrounded in today's competitive, research-conscious, academic society. Teachers do not always have the time or financial support to pursue large-scale PD projects. There is a real dichotomy with PD in the teaching profession, because as a workplace it is geared primarily to produce a product, which in this case is the student experience, and not to produce learning for the workers (Illeris, 2007). The teacher's learning is a very useful and necessary by-product of maintaining currency, but it is not inherently the focus of the job. Also, the act of admitting that teachers in higher education can benefit from professional development with regards to learning and teaching can in itself be seen as a risk. Those with low self-efficacy for learning and adopting new approaches in their teaching can be nervous that undertaking development activities leaves them exposed to an interpretation of having deficiency or a weakness, and as a result these people will work to avoid situations where failure is possible. A teacher with a strong sense of self-efficacy for learning and teaching will view PD as a challenge and an opportunity to improve and deepen practices. Such teachers will plan, use strategic thinking and any available resources to help them learn and succeed in their goals.

With a culture of learning among colleagues and students, the processes of learning alongside teaching becomes not only an enhancement for the teacher, but also a path of mentorship for the students that demonstrates and models learning that is parallel to their own student experience. Experiential real-life development is exactly the same type of learning students undertake in their courses as they explore resources and concepts, deal with different forms of assessment, and prepare to implement skills and knowledge in practical situations. I discuss this with my students when working on research publications, and they see the grief of revisions, or the challenge of tracking down tricky references or having difficulty putting a certain section into writing. This is exposing as an academic, but shows that as a person and a learner I am open to the same challenges as they are. Moreover, it allows students to watch as the journey progresses and to see perseverance and resilience modelled. They see the self-efficacy journey that I undertake and can relate to it vicariously, comparing it to their own learning as they study, reflect, and write for coursework and assessments. Jobs change, but learning continues, and realising that unifies both learner and professional through common ground. Part of enabling a cycle that builds self-efficacy is allowing one's self to become a part of it.

> **...thinking about it**
>
> ► How do you continue learning, whether in public or private, and do you actively reflect on the stages and process that you go through?
> ► Are you aware of how you meet goals, and do you let this experience build your sense of self-efficacy?

Flexibility and growth

During their time in higher education teachers present and explore a range of topics with students; some of these are at a more introductory level and others are in depth. All learning relates and contributes to an accumulating knowledge and expertise. After graduating, it is unlikely that anyone will enter a professional environment that is exactly tailored to the type of learning and the subject matter that has been delivered and studied through a degree programme. People need a degree of adaptability in how they approach the application of studies in life situations beyond the context of education. For example, the student who studied astrophysics may be offered a job working in the stock market, or in computer programming, and there are close relationships between the mathematical principles in these fields, but the transfer of skills is not automatic. That graduate needs to have well-founded self-efficacy beliefs, alongside the skill to recognise the relationships and make the connections to be successful in a new professional future.

Considering a sample of over 300,000 graduates from higher education institutions in the UK in 2006, 50 percent of students who studied creative or artistic subjects secured employment in non-creative jobs (Comunian, Faggian, & Li, 2010). Specific settings certainly vary among different subject areas and specialisms, but there are very few life pursuits where students can expect to carry on doing exactly what they have learned in higher education in exactly the same way. Even within the medical profession, where a high degree of specialisation is undertaken in learning and specifically relates to the professional workplace, only 54 percent of graduating doctors remained in a career that matched their training choices as made when they entered their first year of higher education (Goldacre, Laxton, & Lambert, 2010). Career paths that are directly related to studies still require a strong sense of self-efficacy; otherwise a young professional is likely to flounder.

The concept of being adaptable has direct relevance for teachers as well: professional teachers in higher education each have their own specialist area of expertise, which was most likely not a major in 'how to teach in higher education'. Those who do study education as a degree path specialise either in primary or secondary education, and there is not a direct career progression from teaching in a school environment to teaching in higher education. In this sense, the teachers in higher education need to be aware of their self-efficacy, their skills, and how to approach applying and improving on these in the practical setting. It is unrealistic to expect to step out of a degree and use it as it is. It is one of the jobs that somehow people are expected to already know how to do, and they learn as they go. There are so many variables in teaching, from changes with student numbers and each cohort of different personalities to the landscape within the subject area, considering both physical and technological changes that occur constantly.

Three examples: Music, photography, mythology-folklore

The current Head of the Music and Media department at the University of Chichester is a very effective leader and supportive manager with a keen sense of vision and strategy. Under his guidance and management the department has grown by a factor of ten – truly exponential growth. However, despite his skill as a manager, the 'head of department' job profile bears very little resemblance to the subject matter he spent more than a decade refining as a student in higher education. He was trained to be a professional concert pianist. Because of his adaptability, he recognised the malleability of the skill sets for these two jobs, and how they could be related and one could develop out of the other. He already had very intuitive interpersonal skills and his training within a chamber music setting gave him extensive experience with varying styles of teamwork, where people play independent roles but work seamlessly together. He cultivated this first within the new context of being a teacher in higher education, working with students. This allowed him to develop as an educator, and he then moved forward again as a department head and manager who works with staff and facilitates a team of leaders. This transference of skills is not uncommon, and as Oakley, Sperry, Pratt, and Bakhshi (2008) acknowledged, '" crossover" takes place throughout artists' lives' (p.6). A solid understanding and perception of learning processes and secure beliefs in personal capabilities to learn, grow, and achieve are tools to use with a given skill set to learn, analyse, develop new skills, and establish a successful career in a changing professional landscape.

Each subject has great value for its core body of information, and as a foundation students must still become fluent in the rudimental, cornerstone knowledge that becomes the brickwork to build future careers. It is not an end, not a direct path into a guaranteed vocation. With fast-paced change in technological tools and how they impact social interactions in society, there must be something else that students are getting in higher education beside their skills and knowledge. A strong awareness of their capabilities and a positive sense of self-efficacy for growth and learning within their chosen fields is a skill that will drive them forward in the future.

Having achieved mastery in various tasks within the discipline, the skills then develop for how to understand a novel, and perhaps unrelated, situation and go forward in a way that enables success. Remembering that someone with self-efficacy will use strategies that ensure they do not fail, even in the face of difficulties (Zimmerman, 2000), requires the use of a combination of personal attributes that helps that person to succeed. If the professional landscape is not clear, then they must carve a place for themselves, and with self-belief, self-regulation, and a command of learning strategies, this is possible. An example of students who looked outside to find their own way through using skill and belief are Genea Bailey and Daisy Ware-Jarrett, who, alongside coursework, developed and transferred skills into a context that was beyond what was taught in class. These two students co-developed *Hashtag Magazine*, an Internet-based photography journal that has gained an audience of over 5,000,000 viewers in its two-year existence. They experienced the methodology taught by Jonathan Worth (see Chapter 1 and Chapter 5) of not having an end goal of producing the physical photograph as an 'artefact', and they took this into a new realm. They in turn designed a completely digital magazine that embodied this concept and became a functional and successful outward-facing product.

By making the outcome into a moving target, they were not bound by what is suitable practice for today. They were not being 'rear-view' people (McLuhan & Fiore, 1967) and harkening back to the way things have always been done even though new learning or technology affords new possibilities. They looked at the task and their skills afresh and this gave them new possibilities. What is a sustainable practice for a 21st-century photographer is never going to be static. It is, and always is, going to change, and so there is a need to continually evolve. This forward-thinking mentality seems more urgent in some disciplines than others, but it does affect all students and teachers. Without the critical underlying self-belief in learning that allows both planned and spontaneous adaptation, people will not be leaders but will remain as observers of this development as someone else has the vision and belief to achieve new things. As teachers, we are not preparing students for today's problems, but for tomorrow's possibilities.

In learning, connection facilitates this and the teacher is no longer the central focus point. This shift in perspective, moving from the teacher to the student, is paramount in higher education and was highlighted by Dr Connor (2014) when discussing the UK Professional Standards Framework, which has become a benchmarking tool for professionals in the UK, and saying it is 'about good teaching practice and putting the experience of students first'. This happens when higher education is about the student, and this is facilitated and perpetuated when each student is allowed to connect to everyone else. Instead of having knowledge radiate from a single central point with the teacher; the web of interaction, understanding, and experience passes through and involves each of the participants, including students, teachers, and those around them. When the teacher encourages this connection and becomes a part of it, the facilitation of a connected and co-learning environment becomes a reality (CLA, 2014b). From teachers, this requires them to relinquish some of the traditional authority in a classroom, and students then take responsibility not only for their assignments, but also for the processes, preparation, and even sometimes the content within a class.

Laura Gibbs instructs Mythology-Folklore Online at the University of Oklahoma and has taught in a connected way since 2002 (see http://www.mythfolklore.net/3043mythfolklore/ to access the course). There is a culture of choice and active engagement throughout her course. Gibbs has found a way to circumvent the pressure and prominence of traditional exams, and she grades through creative portfolio work. She is another example of someone who has demonstrated resilience, adaptability, and innovation throughout her career, starting with her own training and carving a path in the professional world of education. With an M-phil from Oxford, she pragmatically admitted that as a specialist subject, 'Bilingual Polish-Latin Renaissance poetry does not indicate a clear career path!' (Gibbs, 2013). Having considerable experience with innovation, Gibbs has used working online to dissolve the traditional hierarchy in present between the teacher and students in education and in turn to empower students with 'real tools' to make their own connections (Gibbs, 2014). These tools can be student's blogs or social media like Twitter, and these are preferred to the learning management systems provided by many institutions because she hopes not only to facilitate the connection within the members of the class, but for students to use these tools for their other work and pursuits as well.

> I want them to make choices about the work they do in class based on their own priorities and interests … hoping to get them to imagine the ways in which what they are doing in school can help be part of their future lives in a positive, creative way. (Gibbs, 2014)

The student's perception of the opportunities for reflection in connected learning come from a range of vantage points, but importantly they are related to them. The focus of learning is on the student, while retaining the goals of meaningful learning, understanding, and a secure academic knowledge base, and this focus gives the student agency to take the learning forward. Although not every teacher will be comfortable with the level of online engagement or autonomy that Laura Gibbs embraces, no education system can unlearn the Internet, un-give the books in the library, or take away the connectedness that exists in society today, but teachers can shift perspectives as to what these tools are for. When learning, especially with anything 'new', whether technology or experience, there can be a fear of not necessarily knowing where the endpoint is. Using what is known and familiar to students to link to and approach new learning is a way of both reducing the gap between distant goals and gaining trust in learning. Proximal goals and incremental tasks create situations where students are likely and capable of succeeding (Bandura, 1993), and this will positively impact their self-efficacy beliefs. A positive dynamic creates trust, and creates a cycle of believing, experimenting, and engaging with learning and arriving at accomplishment.

► Continuing cycles

Teachers can benefit from developing an array of complex new skills, but also from strengthening and concentrating on their teaching skills, because even with extensive specialist knowledge they may not have ever had the time or opportunity to consciously develop their teaching in the setting of higher education. Just as with students, there are processes, and learning and performing are very different; a strong bank of knowledge does not necessarily equate to being good at teaching. Self-efficacy beliefs are specific and a strong belief in one area will not necessarily transfer to another. Even though the skill may exist, there are still confounding intra- and extra-personal factors that will contribute to the practical self-efficacy beliefs for specific tasks.

This is an area of research that needs to be pursued across disciplines, to explore different degrees of transfer and to find evidence for the ways in which self-efficacy beliefs transfer between tasks and settings. Learners find themselves in this situation regularly in taught situations. Teachers also experience this sense of newness when approaching a new class, approaching a new topic, or changing a method of presentation or delivery in their teaching. The process can be surprising, and it can have either a very positive or negative impact on the person's self-efficacy beliefs, depending on whether or not there is preparation, awareness, and understanding of the processes at hand. Even if the person is accomplished as an educator, for self-efficacy beliefs to be relevant and transfer to new situations, he or she needs to perceive and understand how the skills involved directly relate. If someone is in a new situation and the skills do compare, but they are unable to see this, then he or she will suffer from lower self-efficacy, and as a result the performance of the task will suffer.

A practical way to explore how learning on the job happens, in a safe environment, is if teachers place themselves in the student's shoes. Experiencing the student's learning process is not unlike what happens when a teacher begins to teach. There are new situations, new variables, and new skills to learn. By taking on the student's perspective, a teacher is removed from the daily routine to externalise the perspective, and this can be related back to reflections on their own learning processes in teaching.

When the teacher sits the exam

This year, to study my own learning and test and experience self-efficacy beliefs and their development afresh, I decided to undertake what would be a completely new experience for me, but something that was routinely required and undertaken by my students: a formal, graded music exam. Every year hundreds of thousands of students in the UK and across the globe take music performance examinations that are graded by instrument, style, and difficulty. An independent examiner listens and provides numerical scores and supporting written comments for each required component of the exam. Students are required to present various technical exercises and perform a selection of musical pieces that are chosen from a predetermined list for each instrument and grade level. In becoming a student, my task was to experience the task authentically, and a Grade 4 popular music vocal exam was my task. I had never taken a graded music exam, and with the popular music exam, the physicality, timing, speech, and presentation of the whole performance is taken into account, not only the sound, which is different to the classical music exams.

Someone can give a concert and perform with great confidence as a trained musician, appearing secure in their capabilities to play their instrument, and knowing, through experience, how to communicate with the listener in a way that will allow them to be drawn into the performance experience as a comfortable audience member. There may still be nerves, but this is often a sense of excitement and anticipation rather than a detrimental sentiment of worry or anxiety. If, however, someone is taken out of their area of expertise and presented with a novel task, where they have little or no experience, then all of the characteristics of the situation and of the task can potentially challenge the sense of self-efficacy for that person.

As a classically trained cellist, the musical understanding and skill required for the task was well within my capabilities for this intermediate-level singing exam; however, it was still a significant challenge. There was no possibility of knowing the material and shying away from a convincing delivery, because this was a requisite part of the task. Considering the instrument (voice), style, specific task, and setting were new; it was a definite challenge, and as the exam approached, it was tricky for me to see the direct correlation and transfer my existing skill set as a classical cellist to this new situation.

A 'dress rehearsal' of the exam material was presented to a class of undergraduate music students studying instrumental and vocal teaching. Carrying out any new task can be a challenge, and when I stood in front of the class for the first time to sing to them, they were astonished at my nerves and general insecurity with the physicality of this new task. The actual prepared material was adequate, but the delivery was very insecure. The students were shocked that something could rattle the teacher. Becoming aware of the confounding variables of moving between stylistic settings of classical and pop music highlighted the need to consider self-efficacy in this new context. Self-efficacy is as relevant to the teacher as it is to the student, and the perception and security of these beliefs greatly influence the development of learning and performing.

This was the first time I had carried out this task, and there was a craving to receive feedback and reassurance from those observing. It was such a strong feeling that there was a temptation to stop and break character to ask the class what they thought of the processes being observed, and without any interaction the performance became more difficult to maintain as the stalemate of blank stares continued from the onlookers. While standing up and singing to the class, I was unable to adequately judge the success of the performance, because the normal criteria that would be associated with a performance were missing, and without experience, there were no past accomplishments to project forward.

In a teaching situation, the teacher might receive little or no feedback at all from the students as to how they perceive what is happening during a new or challenging teaching session. The default student position is to be receptive in school; they are not expecting to present feedback to the teacher, except perhaps on an evaluation form. This does not lessen the need for the teacher to receive feedback, because this enables reflection and the formation of solid judgements about the success of daily teaching tasks. The interactive and cyclic nature of communication both affirms and guides the progress of the tasks forward.

When taking on something new, it is related either to past experience or to something else that is perceived as being similar. In this case study, preparing for and presenting singing material for a formal music exam was associated with performing in a concert. Although there was no experience with taking a music exam, the situation was assumed to be similar as both contained the direct delivery of musical material. This is correct in some ways, but an exam is very different to a concert setting mainly because there is no audience feedback or interaction. In both settings the musician must perform. Unlike in a concert, the listener's faces did not show anything at all. There was no rapport, response, or feedback, and that was a factor that I had not prepared for. In other performing experiences people did outwardly show signs of enjoyment, but this was within the setting of a formal professional concert, not an exam. The two settings did not directly compare, and because of the lack of understanding of the task itself, there was a lack of preparation for this new, sterile examination setting.

After the singing performance, the experience was discussed with the class, from both the point of view of the observers and the performer.

> How could you be nervous? You were singing Joni Mitchell to us!
> We weren't bored – I really enjoyed that.

Correcting that false association before the assessment took place was important and ensured there could be an accurate perception of self-efficacy beliefs. This made a significant, positive difference in approaching the task of performing in the exam setting.

Both the experience of singing to the class and the discussion afterwards were invaluable parts of the learning and preparation process. Although I was nervous and uncertain at the time, that first foray with the task was carried out and there was a full delivery of the prepared exam material. There was a noticeable lack of comfort with the physical aspects, and the flair of a secure, confident performance was missing, but the fact that this was a practice meant there was time to reflect and improve. If that were the exam in front of a critical audience or assessor instead of a practice in front of a class, self-efficacy beliefs and the outcome of the task would certainly have suffered. Instead, I had the chance to internalise the process and the combined factors of preparation, uncertainty, the delivery in the room, the presence of a listener, and any reaction (or not) that they may have. Understanding the differences between this specific examination task and any other music experiences ensured an informed self-efficacy judgement.

The process highlighted the importance of what are sometimes considered as lesser influences on self-efficacy: communicated persuasion or feedback and physiological signals. Although receiving feedback and some form of affirmation that attributions are being correctly made for aspects of a task can seem basic, especially for someone who is already a professional in another area, but when a task is new these are very important. With support in place to ensure that perceptions and reflection are accurate, external judgements of capability are far more realistic and this is an important step towards enabling a truly confident and assured performance, specifically in an exam setting for this example, but also for any delivery or performance of a new task.

Choosing progress

Self-efficacy beliefs are not permanently static. There have been no longitudinal studies to date of higher education teachers' self-efficacy for their capacity to learn and enact positive changes in their work, nor have there been studies of the specific impact of co-learning models on self-efficacy. Klassen and Chiu (2010) carried out a longitudinal study on school teachers and found that their self-efficacy beliefs did change over the span of their career; teachers who had an excess of 20 years experience had 85 percent stronger self-efficacy beliefs for the use of their teaching strategies than new teachers, and at the end of their careers as motivation waned, there was a dip in self-efficacy beliefs. I conjecture that with stasis there will be regression of self-efficacy beliefs over time for anyone. Firstly, proximity to a task is essential for the most accurate perception of self-efficacy beliefs (Bong, 2006), and secondly, nothing stays the same. Especially in education, where policy, content, cohorts, facilities, and end goals all change regularly and with increasing speed in today's society. To maintain accurate and realistic judgements of self-efficacy that support people achieving successfully, there need to be solid self-efficacy beliefs alongside the skills needed to carry out the tasks (Collins, 1982). With periods of stagnancy between accomplishments, there is time and opportunity for skill to dwindle and become less current. In disciplines that require fine motor control or physical performance, the loss of physical tone and precision affects the delivery of skill, and although less visible in more cognitively based subjects, mental acuity is equally demanding and cannot be left unexercised.

Choosing progress requires a drive to continue and improve, and it does not happen without a concerted effort. Teachers need to go beyond what they have experienced in school and what they were taught, and look wider than the four walls that contain the everyday room. As teachers become more experienced, they rely less on the physical resources in the learning environment to make self-efficacy judgements (Tschannen-Moran, & Hoy, 2007). Looking within to see how teachers can personally develop, learn, and accomplish tasks will lead to enabling themselves and others to become perhaps more than they can see, and is one way teachers can excel and ensure that students take an active role in their learning in higher education and towards their futures. It takes a risk to become the model, especially when the destination is not quite clear and the path is challenging. By reaching out to others, colleagues who are more senior and junior, students, and members of the community, teachers can form collaborations.

Investigations into excellent teaching practices can happen on a local and daily basis as well as through international partnerships. Within teaching, focusing on the processes and looking beyond the immediate criterial boundaries of tasks to see how the underlying skills relate to continuing development for us and for the students, frees educators to develop as professionals and encourage students to grow into capable innovative learners.

As a teaching professional, the impetus for change must come from within to seek, ask, and pursue the challenges. Some will find mentors, and others will have times when they feel that there is nobody external to help with the learning – that they are on their own. Self-efficacy is sustained and developed through resilient teachers who perpetuate and reinforce beliefs in their capabilities, looking forward to accomplishments and goals. Teachers who choose to continue learning and *become students* make active progress, and adopting problem-based approaches to learning makes links to the life-long learning agenda (Brew, 2006).

When teachers choose to continue as learners, they have many of the same challenges and experiences that their students have. They also have the same successes: 'I feel more and more confident about the amount of learning that goes on in my classes ... both my own learning AND the students' learning' (Gibbs, 2014). Using more authentic tasks in the teaching setting develops student self-efficacy, but this ideal necessitates the adaptability of the teacher and a move away from solely traditional modes of teaching and assessment (van Dinther, Dochy, & Segers, 2011).

Building support networks through face-to-face interactions with colleagues and reaching out to the teaching community online provides relevant and useful links with peers. With any new learning, seeing the component steps and analysing, linking together, and adopting effective and efficient strategies will enable a teacher to benefit from the processes of learning as well as the outcomes of their experience. Especially in the teaching profession, experiencing and understanding a situation from multiple perspectives, as a learner, as a teacher, and as a person will lead to deeper understandings of interactions in and out of the learning space.

Examples within this book have been drawn from practical settings within higher education and are a small representation of countless possible examples of excellence, of creativity, and of people who strive to enhance their students' self-efficacy across the academic profession. It is essential to make connections: reflecting on personal practices, evaluating students' experiences, and looking to colleagues not only within a discipline, but across disciplines and institutions for sources of new ideas and practices. Resilient, self-efficacious people, both students and teachers, are equipped to continue developing well beyond the years in formal education. These are the people who will envisage and guide innovative practice for the future.

References

Abdullah, F., Ward, R., Catterall, S., Hill, P., & Wilson, D. (2013). An investigation of the factors that influence engagement with CPD within e-portfolios used for accredited Higher Education course. In Proceedings of Computing and Engineering Annual Researchers' Conference 2013: CEARC '13. University of Huddersfield, Huddersfield, 80–86.

ACT (2011). ACT profile report–national: Graduating class 2011–national. Iowa City, IA: Author. Retrieved from: http://www.act.org/newsroom/data/2011/pdf/profile/National2011.pdf.

ACT (2012). Predicting long-term college success through degree completion using ACT® composite score, ACT benchmarks, and high school grade point average. Iowa City, IA: Author. Retrieved from: http://media.act.org/documents/ACT_RR2012-5.pdf.

Alderman, M. K. (1999). *Motivation for achievement: Possibilities for teaching and learning.* Mahwah, NJ: Erlbaum.

Atkinson, M. (2004). *Lend me your ears: All you need to know about making speeches and presentations.* London: Random House.

Austin, J., Renwick, J., & McPherson, G. E. (2006). Developing motivation. In G. E. McPherson (Ed.) *The child as musician* (pp.213–38). Oxford: Oxford University Press.

Babad, E. (2009). Teaching and nonverbal behavior in the classroom. In *International handbook of research on teachers and teaching* (pp.817–27). US: Springer.

Bandura, A. (1977). Self-efficacy: Toward a unifying theory of behavioral change. *Psychological Review, 84,* 191–215.

Bandura, A. (1984). Recycling misconceptions of perceived self-efficacy. *Cognitive Therapy and Research, 8,* 231–55.

Bandura, A. (1986). *Social foundations of thought and action: A social cognitive theory.* Englewood Cliffs, NJ: Prentice-Hall.

Bandura, A. (1993). Perceived self-efficacy in cognitive development and functioning. *Educational Psychologist, 28*(2), 117–48.

Bandura, A. (1997). *Self-efficacy: The exercise of control.* New York: Freeman.

Bandura, A. (2006). Guide for constructing self-efficacy scales. In F. Pajares & T. Urdan (Eds) *Self-efficacy beliefs of adolescents* (Vol. 5, pp.307–37). Greenwich, CT: Information Age Publishing.

Bandura, A., Barbaranelli, C., Caprara, G. V., & Pastorelli, C. (2001). Self-efficacy beliefs as shapers of children's aspirations and career trajectories. *Child Development, 72,* 187–206.

Bandura, A., & Cervone, D. (1986). Differential engagement of self-reactive influences in cognitive motivation. *Organizational Behavior and Human Decision Processes, 38,* 92–113.

Bandura, A., & Dweck, C. (1988). The relationship of conceptions of intelligence and achievement goals to achievement-related cognition, affect and behaviour. Unpublished manuscript, Harvard University.

Bandura, A., & Jordan, F. (1991). Self-regulatory mechanisms governing the impact of social comparison on complex decision making. *Journal of Personality and Social Psychology, 56,* 805–14.

Bensimon, E. M. (2007). The underestimated significance of practitioner knowledge in the scholarship on student success. *The Review of Higher Education, 30*(4), 441–69.

Benwell, B. (1999). The organisation of knowledge in British university tutorial discourse: Issues, pedagogic discourse strategies and disciplinary identity. *Pragmatics, 9*(4), 535–65.

Blank, R. K., De las Alas, N., & Smith, C. (2008). *Does teacher professional development have effects on teaching and learning?: Analysis of evaluation findings from programs for mathematics and science teachers in 14 states.* Washington, DC: Council of Chief State School Officers.

Bong, M. (2001). Role of self-efficacy and task-value in predicting college students' course performance and future enrollment intentions. *Contemporary Educational Psychology, 26*(4), 553–70.

Bong, M. (2006). Asking the right questions. In F. Pajares & T. C. Urdan (Eds) *Self-efficacy beliefs of adolescents* (pp.287–305). Greenwich, CT: Information Age Publishing.

Bong, M., & Clark, R. (1999). Comparison between self-concept and self-efficacy in academic motivation research. *Educational Psychologist, 34*, 139–53.

Boore, J. (1993). Teaching standards from quality circles. In R. Ellis (Ed.) *Quality assurance for university teaching* (pp.194–210). Buckingham: Open University Press.

Bouffard-Bouchard, T. (1990). Influence of self-efficacy on performance in a cognitive task. *Journal of Social Psychology, 130*, 353–63.

Boyer Commission (1999). *Reinventing undergraduate education: A blueprint for America's research universities.* Carnegie Foundation for the Advancement of Teaching. State University of New York, Stony Brook.

Bresnahan, T. (2012). Large classes: Keeping the energy in 220 relationships at once [video file]. Retrieved from: https://www.youtube.com/watch?v=OzF2GRmkW0o&feature=youtu.be.

Brew, A. (2006). *Research and teaching beyond the divide.* Basingstoke: Palgrave Macmillan.

Bridgstock, R. (2009). The graduate attributes we've overlooked: Enhancing graduate employability through career management skills. *Higher Education Research & Development, 28*(1), 31–44.

Brockbank, A., & McGill, I. (2007). *Facilitating reflective learning in higher education.* New York: McGraw-Hill International.

Campbell, G. (26 July 2008). The Reverend asked me a question [Internet file]. Retrieved from: http://www.gardnercampbell.net/blog1/?p=620.

CES (2009). *The employability challenge.* London: UK Commission for Employment and Skills. Retrieved from: http://www.employability.ed.ac.uk/documents/Staff/PoliciesReports/UKCES-EmployabilityChallenge-ExecSum-Feb2009.pdf.

Cleary, T. J., & Zimmerman, B. J. (2001). Self-regulation differences during athletic practice by experts, non-experts, and novices. *Journal of Applied Sport Psychology, 13*, 185–206.

Collins, J. (1982). Self-efficacy and ability in achievement behaviour. In Annual meeting of the American Educational Research Association. March, New York.

Comunian, R., Faggian, A., & Li, Q. C. (2010). Unrewarded careers in the creative class: The strange case of bohemian graduates. *Papers in Regional Science, 89*(2), 389–410.

Connected Learning Alliance (2014a). Why does #ConnectedLearning emphasize 'production-centered' activity? [infographic tweet] Retrieved from: https://twitter.com/TheCLAlliance/status/545013216687185920.

Connected Learning Alliance (2014b). Connected learning: The power of making learning relevant [video file]. Retrieved from: http://vimeo.com/98763656.

Connor, C. (2014). UKPSF [webpage]. Retrieved from: https://www.heacademy.ac.uk/.

Cousin, G. (2006). An introduction to threshold concepts. *Planet, 17*, 4–5.

Cowan, J. (2006). *On becoming an innovative university teacher: Reflection in action.* New York: McGraw-Hill International.

Darling-Hammond, L. (2008). Teacher learning that supports student learning. *Teaching for Intelligence*, *2*, 91–100.

Daunert, A. L., & Price, L. (2014). E-Portfolio: A practical tool for self-directed, reflective, and collaborative professional learning. In C. Harteis, A. Rausch, & J. Seifried (Eds) *Discourses on professional learning* (pp.231–51). Dordrecht, The Netherlands: Springer.

Day, R., & Allen, T. D. (2004). The relationship between career motivation and self-efficacy with protégé career success. *Journal of Vocational Behavior*, *64*(1), 72–91.

Deveugele, M., Derese, A., Maesschalck, S. D., Willems, S., Driel, M. V., & Maeseneer, J. D. (2005). Teaching communication skills to medical students, a challenge in the curriculum? *Patient Education and Counseling*, *58*(3), 265–70.

DMV (2014). Driver's training [webpage]. Retrieved from: http://www.dmv.org/drivers-training.php.

Dunkin, M. J., & Precians, R. P. (1992). Award-winning university teachers' concepts of teaching. *Higher Education*, *24*(4), 483–502.

Eales, J. (2011). Recognising excellence: University of Exeter Students' Guild teaching awards. *Guardian Education*, 14 November. Retrieved from: http://www.theguardian.com/higher-education-network/blog/2011/nov/14/teaching-awards-university-of-exeter.

Eccles, J. S. (2005). Subjective task value and the Eccles et al. model of achievement-related choices. In A. J. Elliot & C. S. Dweck (Eds) *Handbook of competence and motivation* (pp.105–21). New York: Guilford Press.

Eccles, J., Adler, J., & Meece, J. (1984). Sex differences in achievement: A test of alternate theories. *Journal of Personality and Social Psychology*, *46*, 26–43.

Eccles, J. S., & Wigfield, A. (2002). Motivational beliefs, values, and goals. *Annual Review of Psychology*, *53*(1), 109–32.

Ehiyazaryan, E. (2012). The dialogic potential of e-Portfolios – Formative feedback and communities of learning within a personal learning environment. *International Journal of ePortfolio*, *2*(2). Retrieved from: http://www.theijep.com/current.cfm.

Ertmer, P. A., Newby, T. J., & MacDougall, M. (1996). Students' responses and approaches to case-based instruction: The role of reflective self-regulation. *American Educational Research Journal*, *33*(3), 719–52.

Feden, P. (2012). Teaching without telling: Contemporary pedagogical theory put into practice. *Journal of Excellence in College Teaching*, *23*, 5–23.

Feltz, D., Chow, G., & Hepler, T. (2006). Path analysis of self-efficacy and performance: Revisited. *Journal of Sport and Exercise Psychology*, *28*, S66.

Ferguson, P. (2011). Student perceptions of quality feedback in teacher education. *Assessment & Evaluation in Higher Education*, *36*(1), 51–62.

Finkel, E. J., & Fitzsimons, G. M. (2011). The effects of social relationships on self-regulation. In K. D. Vohs & R. F. Baumeister (Eds) *Handbook of self-regulation: Research, theory, and applications* (2nd Ed., pp.390–406). New York: Guilford Press.

Flavell, J. H. (1985). *Cognitive development* (2nd Ed.). Englewood Cliffs, NJ: Prentice-Hall.

Garcia, T., & Pintrich, P. R. (1994). Regulating motivation and cognition in the classroom: The role of self-schemas and self-regulatory strategies. In D. Schunk & B. J. Zimmerman (Eds) *Self-regulation of learning and performance: Issues and educational applications* (pp.127–53). Hillsdale, NJ: Lawrence Erlbaum.

Gaunt, H. (2008). One-to-one tuition in a conservatoire: The perceptions of instrumental and vocal teachers. *Psychology of Music*, *36*(2), 215–45.

Gerstein, J. (2014). Moving from education 1.0 through education 2.0 towards education 3.0. In L. M. Blaschke, C. Kenyon, & S. Hase (Eds) *Experiences in self-determined learning* (pp.83–98). Scotts Valley, CA: CreateSpace Independent Publishing Platform.

Gibb, A., & Haskins, G. (2014). The university of the future: An entrepreneurial stake-holder learning organisation? In. A. Fayolle & D. T. Redford (Eds) *Handbook on the entrepreneurial university* (pp.25–63). Cheltenham: Edward Elgar Publishing.

Gibbs, G., & Coffey, M. (2004). The impact of training of university teachers on their teaching skills, their approach to teaching and the approach to learning of their students. *Active Learning in Higher Education, 5*(1), 87–100.

Gibbs, L. (2013). Laura Gibbs: Something about me [webpage]. http://onlinecourselady .pbworks.com/w/page/12783437/aboutme.

Gibbs, L. (2014). Unpublished interview. 21 December, 2014.

Goldacre, M. J., Laxton, L., & Lambert, T. W. (2010). Medical graduates' early career choices of specialty and their eventual specialty destinations: UK prospective cohort studies. *British Medical Journal, 341.*

Greene, B., & Miller, R. (1996). Influences on achievement: Goals, perceived ability, and cognitive engagement. *Contemporary Educational Psychology, 21,* 181–92.

Greenlees, I. A., Nunn, R. L., Graydon, J. K., & Maynard, I. W. (1999). The relationship between collective efficacy and precompetitive affect in rugby players: Testing Bandura's model of collective efficacy. *Perceptual and motor skills, 89*(2), 431–40.

Guerrero, L. K., & Floyd, K. (2006). *Nonverbal communication in close relationships.* Mahwah, NJ: Laurence Erlbaum.

Hallam, S. (1998). *Instrumental teaching: A practical guide to better teaching and learning.* Oxford: Heinemann.

Hallam, S. (2001). The development of expertise in young musicians: Strategy use, knowledge acquisition and individual diversity. *Music Education Research, 3,* 7–23.

Hanton, S., & Jones, G. (1999). The acquisition and development of cognitive skills and strategies: I. Making the butterflies fly in formation. *The Sport Psychologist, 13,* 1–21.

Hanton, S., O'Brien, M., & Mellalieu, S. D. (2003). Individual differences, perceived control and competitive trait anxiety. *Journal of Sport Behavior, 26*(1), 39–55.

Hartmann, T. V. (2012). Interview with photographer Jonathan Worth [video file]. Retrieved from: http://www.statedmag.com/articles/interview-jonathan-worth-photographer-and-open-source-online.html/#.

Hattie, J., Biggs, J., & Purdie, N. (1996). Effects of learning skills interventions on student learning: A meta-analysis. *Review of Educational Research, 66*(2), 99–136.

HEA (2014). *Framework for partnership in learning and teaching in higher education.* York: Higher Education Academy.

Heron, J. (1985). The role of reflection in a co-operative inquiry. In D. Boud, R. Keogh, & D. Walker (Eds) *Reflection: Turning experience into learning* (pp.128–38). London: Kogan Page.

Higgins, S., Hall, E., Wall, K., Woolner, P., & McCaughey, C. (2005). The impact of school environments: A literature review. The Centre for Learning and Teaching, School of Education, Communication and Language Science, University of Newcastle.

Hillier, Y. (2002). The quest for competence, good practice and excellence. Retrieved from: www.heacademy.ac.uk/resources/detail/id494/quest_for_competence.

Hillier, Y., & Vielba, C., (2001). Perceptions of excellence: Personal constructs of excellence in teaching and learning. Institute of Learning and Teaching Annual Conference, University of York.

Hofer, B. K., Yu, S. L., & Pintrich, P. R. (1998). Teaching college students to be self-regulated learners. In D. H. Schunk & B. J. Zimmerman (Eds) *Self-regulated Learning: From Teaching to Self-reflective Practice,* (pp. 57–85). New York: Guildford Press.

Holmes, K., & Papageorgiou, G. (2009). Good, bad and insufficient: Students' expectations, perceptions and uses of feedback. *Journal of Hospitality Leisure Sport & Tourism Education, 8*(1), 85–96.

Huxham, M. (2007). Fast and effective feedback: Are model answers the answer? *Assessment & Evaluation in Higher Education, 32*(6), 601–11.

Illeris, K. (2007). *How we learn: Learning and non-learning in school and beyond.* Abingdon, New York: Routledge.

Ito, M. (2010). Peer based learning in a networked age [blog post]. Retrieved from: http://www.itofisher.com/mito/publications/peerbased_learn_2.html.

JCQ (2013). GCE results booklet. Retrieved from: http://www.jcq.org.uk/examination-results/a-levels/a-as-and-aea-results-summer-2013.

Jensen, H. Unpublished interview. 6 July 2013.

Jonassen, D. (2013). Designing constructivist learning environments. In C. M. Reigeluth (Ed.) *Instructional-design theories and models: A new paradigm of instructional theory* (Vol. 2, pp.215–40). Mahwah, NJ: Routledge.

Jones, S. E. (2007). Reflections on the lecture: outmoded medium or instrument of inspiration? *Journal of Further and Higher Education, 31*(4), 397–406.

Jordan, F. (1992). The influence of feedback framing on self-regulatory mechanisms: A glass half full or half empty. Unpublished BEBR faculty working paper; no. 93-0117. Champaign, IL: University of Illinois at Urbana-Champaign.

Jørgensen, H. (2000). Student learning in higher instrumental education: Who is responsible? *British Journal of Music Education, 17*(1), 67–77.

Karlsson, J., & Juslin, P. (2008). Musical expression: An observational study of instrumental teaching. *Psychology of Music, 36*(3), 309–34.

Kelly, K. (2008). Better than free [Internet file]. Retrieved from: http://kk.org/thetechnium/2008/01/better-than-fre/.

Klassen, R. M., & Chiu, M. M. (2010). Effects on teachers' self-efficacy and job satisfaction: Teacher gender, years of experience, and job stress. *Journal of Educational Psychology, 102*(3), 741.

Knapp, M. L., & Hall, J. A. (2005). *Nonverbal communication in human interaction* (6th Ed). Belmont, CA: Wadsworth.

Knight, P., & Yorke, M. (2004). *Learning, curriculum and employability in higher education.* London: RoutledgeFalmer.

Kolb, D. A. (1984). *Experiential learning: Experience as the source of learning and development* (Vol. 1). Englewood Cliffs, NJ: Prentice-Hall.

Konstantopolous, S. (1996). Math self-efficacy and intrinsic values as predictors or math performance. In Annual Meeting of the American Educational Research Association. April, New York.

Kuriansky, J. (2014). Martin Luther King Jr. Words of wisdom: Apply to your life [Internet document]. *Huffingpost.* Retrieved from: http://www.huffingtonpost.com/judy-kuriansky-phd/martin-luther-king-jr-wor_b_4624747.html.

Laurillard, D. (2013). *Rethinking university teaching: A conversational framework for the effective use of learning technologies.* London: Routledge.

Lent, R. W., Brown, S. D., & Hackett, G. (2000). Contextual supports and barriers to career choice: A social cognitive analysis. *Journal of Counseling Psychology, 47*(1), 36.

Linnenbrink, E.A., & Pintrich, P.R., (2003). The role of self-efficacy beliefs in student engagement and learning in the classroom. *Reading and Writing Quarterly: Overcoming learning difficulties, 19*(2), 119 –37.

Little, B., Locke, W., Parker, J., & Richardson, J. (2007). *Excellence in teaching and learning: A review of the literature for the Higher Education Academy.* UK: Higher Education Academy.

Lock, E., & Latham, G. (1990). *A theory of goal setting and task performance.* Englewood Cliffs, NJ: Prentice Hall.

LooSE TV (9 May 2012). *Michael Sandel at the LSE.* [video file]. Retrieved from: https://www.youtube.com/watch?v=-yfC-Pvwug.

Lumpe, A., Vaughn, A., Henderson, R., & Bishop, D. (2014). Teacher professional development and self-efficacy beliefs. In R. Evans, J. Luft, C. Czerniak, & C. Pea (Eds) *The role of science teachers' beliefs in international classrooms: From teacher actions to student learning* (pp.49–64). Dordrecht, The Netherlands: Springer.

Lunt, T., & Curran, J. (2010). 'Are you listening please?' The advantages of electronic audio feedback compared to written feedback. *Assessment & Evaluation in Higher Education, 35*(7), 759–69.

Marlina, R. (2009). 'I don't talk or I decide not to talk? Is it my culture?' – International students' experiences of tutorial participation. *International Journal of Educational Research, 48*(4), 235–44.

Martin, P., Katz, T., Morris, R., & Kilgallon, S. (2008). A learning space for creativity: Early findings. In J. Barlow, G. Louw, & M. Price (Eds) *Connections: Sharing the learning space* (pp.13–17). Brighton: University of Brighton Press.

Mazur, E. (2014). Turning lectures into learning [video file]. Retrieved from: https://www.youtube.com/watch?v=dUJS48XQeXE.

McLuhan, M., & Fiore, Q. (1967). *The medium is the massage: An Inventory of Effects.* Co-ordinated by J. Agel. New York, London, Toronto: Bantam Books.

McPherson, G. E., & McCormick, J. (2006). Self-efficacy and music performance. *Psychology of Music, 34*, 332–36.

McPherson, G. E., & Renwick, J. (2001). A longitudinal study of self-regulation in children's music practice. *Music Education Research, 3*, 169–86.

McPherson, G. E., & Schubert, E. (2004). Measuring performance enhancement in music. In A. Williamon (Ed.) *Musical excellence: Strategies and techniques to enhance performance* (pp.61–82). Oxford: Oxford University Press.

McPherson, G. E., & Zimmerman, B. J. (2002). Self-regulation of musical learning: A social cognitive perspective. In R. Colwell & C. Richardson (Eds) *The New handbook of research on music teaching and learning* (pp.327–47). Oxford: Oxford University Press.

Meyer, J. H. F., Land, R., & Davies, P. (2006). Implications of threshold concepts for course design and evaluation. In J. H. F. Meyer & R. Land (Eds) *Overcoming barriers to student understanding: Threshold concepts and troublesome knowledge.* London and New York: Routledge.

Meyer, K. A. (2003). Face-to-face versus threaded discussions: The role of time and higher-order thinking. *Journal of Asynchronous Learning Networks, 7*(3), 55–65.

Morris, D. (1994). *Bodytalk: The meaning of human gestures.* New York: Crown Publishers.

Mullen, C. A. (2011). Facilitating self-regulated learning using mentoring approaches with doctoral students. In. B. J. Zimmerman & D. H. Schunk (Eds) *Handbook of self-regulation of learning and performance* (pp.137–54). New York: Routledge.

Neary, M., & Winn, J. (2009). The student as producer: reinventing the student experience in higher education. In L. Bell, M. Neary, & H. Stevenson (Eds) *The future of higher education: Policy, pedagogy and the student experience* (pp.126–38). London, New York: Continuum International.

Newman, M. (2004). *Problem-based learning: An exploration of the method and evaluation of its effectiveness in a continuing nursing education programme.* London: Middlesex University.

Nicholls, G. (2001). *Professional development in higher education: New dimensions & directions.* London, New York: Psychology Press.

Norton, L., Richardson, J. T. E., Hartley, J., Newstead, S., & Mayes, J. (2005). Teachers' beliefs and Intentions concerning teaching in higher education. *Higher Education, 50*(4), 537–71.

Oakley, K., Sperry, B., Pratt, A. C., & Bakhshi, H. (2008). *The art of innovation: How fine arts graduates contribute to innovation.* London: NESTA.

Pajares, F. (1996a). Self-efficacy beliefs and mathematical problem solving of gifted students. *Contemporary Educational Psychology, 21*, 325–44.

Pajares, F. (1996b). Self-efficacy beliefs in academic settings. *Review of Educational Research, 66*(4), 543–78.

Pajares, F. (1997). Current directions in self-efficacy research. *Advances in Motivation and Achievement, 10*(149), 1–49.

Pajares, F., & Miller, M. (1994). The role of self-efficacy and self-concept beliefs in mathematical problem-solving: A path analysis. *Journal of Educational Psychology, 86*, 193–203.

Pajares, F., & Schunk, D. (2001). The development of academic self-efficacy. In A. Wigfield & J. Eccles (Eds) *Development of achievement motivation* (pp.16–32). London: Academic Press.

Pegg, A., Waldock, J., Hendy-Isaac, S., & Lawton, R. (2012). *Pedagogy for employability.* York: Higher Education Academy. Retrieved from: http://oro.open.ac.uk/30792/4/Pedagogy_for_employability_170212_1724.pdf.

Persson, R. S. (1993). *The subjectivity of musical performance: An exploratory music-psychological real world enquiry into the determinants and education of musical reality* (Doctoral dissertation, University of Huddersfield).

Pintrich, P. R., & Schunk, D. H. (2002). *Motivation in education: Theory, research, and applications* (2nd Ed). Upper Saddle, NJ: Prentice-Hall.

Pitts, S. E. (2005). 'Testing, testing.' How do students use written feedback? *Active Learning in Higher Education, 6*(3), 218–29.

Plante, I., O'Keefe, P. A., & Théorêt, M. (2013). The relation between achievement goal and expectancy-value theories in predicting achievement-related outcomes: A test of four theoretical conceptions. *Motivation and Emotion, 37*(1), 65–78.

Pool, L. D., & Sewell, P. (2007). The key to employability: Developing a practical model of graduate employability. *Education+ Training, 49*(4), 277–89.

Power, D. (1990). The use of audio in distance education. In S. Timmers (Ed.) *Training needs in the use of media for distance education* (pp.43–60). Singapore: Asian Mass Communication Research and Information Centre.

Preston, D. (2013). Open source learning [video file]. TEDx UCLA. Retrieved from: https://www.youtube.com/watch?v=mp0-QQQgv7s.

Preston, D. (2014). Case study: 5ph1nx. In Harold Rhingold (Ed.) *Peeragogy* (2nd Ed. [ebook], pp.49–62). Retrieved from: http://metameso.org/peeragogy-2.01-ebook.pdf .

Power, D. (1990). The use of audio in distance education. In S. Timmers (Ed), *Training needs in the use of media for distance education* (pp. 43–60). Singapore: Asian Mass Communication Research and Information Centre.

Race, P. (2014). *Making learning happen: A guide for post-compulsory education.* London: Sage.

Ramsden, P. (2003). *Learning to teach in higher education.* London: Routledge.

Ramstad, E. (2012). U.S. professor is hit in Seoul. *Wall Street Journal.* 5 June. Retrieved from: http://online.wsj.com/article/SB10001424052702303506404577445841573895570.html

Ribchester, C., France, D., & Wakefield, K. (2008). *'It was just like a personal tutorial': Using podcasts to provide assessment feedback.* July. Paper presented at the Higher Education Academy Conference, York, UK.

Risemberg, R., & Zimmerman, B. (1992). Self-regulated learning in gifted students. *Roper Review, 15*, 98–101.

Ritchie, L., & Kearney, P. (2013). Transfer of practice strategies: From primary to secondary instruments. In A. Williamon & W. Goebl (Eds) *Proceedings of the International Symposium on Performance Science 2013* (pp.111–16). European Association of Conservatoires (AEC).

Ritchie, L., & Kearney, P. (In Preparation). Enhancing self-regulatory processes of adults learning music.

Ritchie, L., & Williamon, A. (2011). Measuring distinct types of musical self-efficacy. *Psychology of Music, 38,* 328–44.

Ritchie, L., & Williamon, A. (2012). Self-efficacy as a predictor of musical performance quality. *Psychology of Aesthetics, Creativity, and Arts, 6*(4), 334–40.

Ruben, B. D. (2007). *Excellence in higher education: An integrated approach to assessment, planning, and improvement in colleges and universities.* Washington: National Association of College and University Business Officers.

Ruiz, J. G., Mintzer, M. J., & Leipzig, R. M. (2006). The impact of E-learning in medical education. *Academic Medicine, 81*(3), 207–12.

Sambell, K., McDowell, L., & Brown, S. (1997). 'But is it fair?' an exploratory study of student perceptions of the consequential validity of assessment. *Studies in Educational Evaluation, 23*(4), 349–71.

Sandel, M. (2014). Michael Sandel: The public philosopher. [Radio broadcast episode] 20 May. London School of Economics and Politics. BBC.

Schaefer, B. E. (1993). Astronomy and the limits of vision. *Vistas in Astronomy, 36,* 311–61.

Schön, D. A. (1987). *Educating the reflective practitioner: Toward a new design for teaching and learning in the professions.* San Francisco, CA: Jossey-Bass.

Schulze, P., & Schulze, J. (2003). Believing is achieving: The implications of self-efficacy research for family and consumer sciences education. In B. L. Stewart, R. S. Purcell, R. P. Lovingood (Eds) *AAFCS Monograph: Research Applications in Family and Consumer Sciences* (pp.105–13). Alexandria, VA: American Association of Family and Consumer Sciences.

Schunk, D. H. (1981). Modelling and attributional effects on children's achievement: A self-efficacy analysis. *Journal of Educational Psychology, 73,* 93–105.

Schunk, D. H. (1989). Self-efficacy and achievement behaviors. *Educational Psychology Review, 1,* 173–208.

Schunk, D. H. (1996a). Self-efficacy for learning and performance. In Annual Meeting of the American Educational Research Association. April, New York.

Schunk, D. H. (1996b). Goal and self-evaluative influences during children's cognitive skill learning. *American Educational Research Journal, 33*(2), 359–82.

Schunk, D. H. (1998). Teaching Elementary students to self-regulate practice of mathematical skills with modeling. In D. H. Schunk & B. J. Zimmerman (Eds) *Self-regulated learning: From teaching to self-reflective practice* (pp.137–59). New York: The Guilford Press.

Schunk, D. H. (2000). *Learning theories.* Upper Saddle, NJ: Prentice Hall.

Schunk, D. H. (2003). Self-efficacy for reading and writing: Influence of modeling, goal setting, and self-evaluation. *Reading & Writing Quarterly, 19*(2), 159–72.

Schunk, D. H., & Ertmer, P. A. (2000). Self-regulation and academic learning: Self-efficacy enhancing interventions. In M. Boekaerts, P. R. Pintrich, & M. Zeidner (Eds) *Handbook of self-regulation* (pp.631–49). San Diego, CA: Academic Press.

Schunk, D. H., & Hanson, A. (1985). Peer models: Influence on children's self-efficacy and achievement. *Journal of Educational Psychology, 77,* 313–22.

Schunk, D. H., & Hanson, A. R. (1989). Influence of peer-model attributes on children's beliefs and learning. *Journal of Educational Psychology, 81*(3), 431.

Schunk, D. H., Hanson, A., & Cox, P. (1987). Peer-model attributes and children's achievement behaviors. *Journal of Educational Psychology, 79,* 54–61.

Schunk, D. H., & Meece, J. L. (2006). Self-efficacy development in adolescence. In. F. Pajares (Ed.) *Self-efficacy beliefs of adolescents* (pp.71–96). Greenwich, CT: Information Age Publishing.

Schunk, D. H., & Mullen, C. A. (2012). Self-efficacy as an engaged learner. In S. Christenson, A. L. Reschley, & C. Wylie (Eds) *Handbook of research on student engagement* (pp.219–35). New York: Springer.

Schunk, D. H., & Pajares, F. (2002). The development of academic self-efficacy. In. A. Wigfield & J. S. Eccles (Eds) *Development of achievement motivation* (pp.18–23). San Diego, CA: Academic Press.

Schunk, D. H., & Pajares, F. (2009). Self-efficacy theory. In K. R. Wentzel & A. Wigfield (Eds) *Handbook of motivation at school* (pp. 35–53). New York: Routledge.

Schunk, D., & Rice, J. (1993). Strategy fading and progress feedback: Effects on self-efficacy and comprehension among students receiving remedial reading services. *Journal of Special Education, 27*, 257–76.

Schunk, D. H., & Usher, E. L. (2011). Assessing self-efficacy for self-regulated learning. In. B. J. Zimmerman & D. H. Schunk (Eds) *Handbook of self-regulation of learning and performance* (pp.282–97). New York: Routledge.

Schunk, D. H., & Usher, E. L. (2012). Social cognitive theory and motivation. In R. Ryan (Ed.) *The Oxford handbook of human motivation* (pp.13–27). New York: Oxford University Press.

Schunk, D. H., & Usher, E. L. (2013). Barry J. Zimmerman's theory of self-regulated learning. In H. Bembenutty, T. Cleary, & A. Kitsantas (Eds) *Applications of self-regulated learning across diverse disciplines: A tribute to Barry J. Zimmerman* (pp.1–28). Charlotte, NY: Information Age Publishing.

Schunk, D. H., & Zimmerman, B. J. (1997). Social origins of self-regulatory competence. *Educational Psychologist, 32*(4), 195–208.

Schunk, D. H., & Zimmerman, B. J. (1998). Conclusions and future directions for academic interventions. In D. H. Schunk & B. J. Zimmerman (Eds) *Self-regulated learning: From teaching to reflective practice* (pp. 225–35). New York: Guildford.

Schunk, D. H., & Zimmerman, B. J. (2007). Influencing children's self-efficacy and self-regulation of reading and writing through modeling. *Reading & Writing Quarterly, 23*(1), 7–25.

Shell, D., Murphy, C., & Bruning, R. (1989). Self-efficacy and outcome expectancy mechanisms in reading and writing achievement. *Journal of Educational Psychology, 81*, 91–100.

Shuell, T. J. (1986). Cognitive conceptions of learning. *Review of Educational Research, 56*(4), 411–36.

Skelton, A. (2005). *Understanding teaching excellence in higher education: Towards a critical approach.* Abingdon: Routledge.

Smith, C., Hofer, J., Gillespie, M., Solomon, M., & Rowe, K. (2006) How teachers change: A study of professional development in adult education. In P. R. Villia (Ed.) *Teacher change and development* (pp.11–155). New York: Nova Science.

Smith, D. J., & Valentine, T. (2012). The use and perceived effectiveness of instructional practices in two-year technical colleges. *Journal on Excellence in College Teaching, 23*(1), 133–61.

Smith, W., & Anthon, C. (Eds) (1843). *A dictionary of Greek and Roman antiquities.* London: John Murray.

Stephenson, J. (2012). Supporting student autonomy in learning. In J. Stephenson & M. Yorke (Eds) *Capability and quality in higher education* (pp.129–41). London: Kogan Page.

Stravinsky, I. (1970). *Poetics of music in the form of six lessons.* Cambridge, MA: Harvard University Press.

Struyven, K., Dochy, F., & Janssens, S. (2008). The effects of hands-on experience on students' preferences for assessment methods. *Journal of Teacher Education, 59*(1), 69–88.

The Quality Assurance Agency for Higher Education (QAA) (2007a). *Subject benchmark statement: English.* Gloucester: QAA.

The Quality Assurance Agency for Higher Education (QAA) (2007b). *Subject benchmark statement: Computing.* Gloucester: QAA.

The Quality Assurance Agency for Higher Education (QAA) (2007c). *Subject benchmark statement: Dance, drama, and performance.* Gloucester: QAA.

The Quality Assurance Agency for Higher Education (QAA) (2008a). *Subject benchmark statement: Art and design.* Gloucester: QAA.

The Quality Assurance Agency for Higher Education (QAA) (2008b). *Subject benchmark statement: Health studies.* Gloucester: QAA.

The Quality Assurance Agency for Higher Education (QAA) (2009). *Subject benchmark statement: Agriculture, horticulture, forestry, food and consumer sciences.* Gloucester: QAA.

The Quality Assurance Agency for Higher Education (QAA) (2012). *Enterprise and entre-preneurship education. Guidance for UK enterprise education providers.* Gloucester: QAA.

The Quality Assurance Agency for Higher Education (QAA) (2014). *Subject benchmark statement: Theology.* Gloucester: QAA.

Thoreson, C., & Mahoney, M. (1974). *Behavioral self-control.* New York: Holt, Rinehart, & Winston.

Timperley, H. S., & Phillips, G. (2003). Changing and sustaining teachers' expectations through professional development in literacy. *Teaching and Teacher Education, 19*(6), 627–41.

Tinto, V., & Pusser, B. (2006). *Moving from theory to action: Building a model of institu-tional action for student success.* Washington, DC: National Postsecondary Education Cooperative.

Tobin, K. (1987). The role of wait time in higher cognitive level learning. *Review of Educational Research, 57*(1), 69–95.

Triantafyllaki, A. (2005). A call for more instrumental music teaching research. *Music Education Research, 7*(3), 383–87.

Tschannen-Moran, M., & Hoy, A. W. (2007). The differential antecedents of self-efficacy beliefs of novice and experienced teachers. *Teaching and Teacher Education, 23*(6), 944–56.

Tschannen-Moran, M., & McMaster, P. (2009). Sources of self-efficacy: Four professional development formats and their relationship to self-efficacy and implementation of a new teaching strategy. *The Elementary School Journal, 110*(2), 228–45.

Turner, S., & Lapan, R. T. (2002). Career self-efficacy and perceptions of parent support in adolescent career development. *The Career Development Quarterly, 51*(1), 44–55.

Tzeng, J. Y., & Cheng, S. H. (2012). College students' intentions to use e-portfolios: From the perspectives of career-commitment status and weblog-publication behaviours. *British Journal of Educational Technology, 43*(1), 163–76.

Urdan, T., & Schoenfelder, E. (2006). Classroom effects on student motivation: Goal structures, social relationships, and competence beliefs. *Journal of School Psychology, 44*(5), 331–49.

Utley, A. (2004). Problem method has high dropout. *The Times Higher Education Supplement.* 28 May, p.13. Retrieved from: http://www.timeshighereducation.co.uk/news/problem-method-has-high-dropout/188968.article.

van Dinther, M., Dochy, F., & Segers, M. (2011). Factors affecting students' self-efficacy in higher education. *Educational Research Review, 6*(2), 95–108.

Vygotsky, L. S. (1978). *Mind in society: The development of higher psychological processes.* Cambridge, MA: Harvard University Press.

Vygotsky, L. S. (1987). *The collected works of LS Vygotsky: Vol. 1, Problems of general psy-chology* (R. W. Rieber & A. S. Carton, Eds). New York, London: Plenum Press.

Wayne, D. B., Butter, J., Siddall, V. J., Fudala, M. J., Wade, L. D., Feinglass, J., & McGaghie, W. C. (2006). Mastery learning of advanced cardiac life support skills by internal medicine residents using simulation technology and deliberate practice. *Journal of General Internal Medicine, 21*(3), 251–56.

Weaver, M. R. (2006). Do students value feedback? Student perceptions of tutors' written responses. *Assessment & Evaluation in Higher Education, 31*(3), 379–94.

Webster-Wright, A. (2010). Authentic professional learning: Making a difference through learning at work. In S. Billett, C. Harteis, & H. Gruber (Eds) *Professional and practiced-based learning* (Vol. 2, pp.107–44). Dordrecht, The Netherlands: Springer.

Wegner, D. M., Schneider, D. J., Carter, S. R., & White, T. L. (1987). Paradoxical effects of thought suppression. *Journal of Personality and Social Psychology, 53*(1), 5.

Weimer, M. (2013). *Learner-centered teaching: Five key changes to practice.* San Francisco, CA: John Wiley & Sons.

Weinstein, C. E., Husman, J., & Dierking, D. R. (2000). Self-regulation interventions with a focus on learning strategies. In M. Boekarts, P. R. Pintrich, & M. Zeidner (Eds) *Handbook of self-regulation* (pp.728–48). San Diego, CA: Academic Press.

Weinstein, C. E. & Acee, T. W. (2013). Helping college students become more strategic and self-regulated learners. In H. Bembenutty, T. J. Cleary, & A. Kitsantas (Eds) *Applications of self-regulated learning across diverse disciplines: A tribute to Barry J. Zimmerman* (pp.197–236). Charlotte, NC: Information Age Publishing.

Wigfield, A., & Eccles, J. S. (1992). The development of achievement task values: A theoretical analysis. *Developmental Review, 12*(3), 265–310.

Wigfield, A., Eccles, J. S., & Pintrich, P. R. (1996). Development between the ages of eleven and twenty-five. In D. C. Berliner & R. C. Calfee (Eds) *The handbook of educational psychology* (pp.148–87). New York: Macmillan.

Wigfield, A., Tonks, S., & Eccles, J. S. (2004). Expectancy-value theory in cross-cultural perspective. In D. M. McInerney & S. Van Etten (Eds) *Research on sociocultural influences on motivation and learning, volume 4: Big theories revisited* (pp.165–98). Greenwich, CT: Information Age Publishing.

Williamon, A. (Ed.) (2004). *Musical excellence: Strategies and techniques to enhance performance.* Oxford: Oxford University Press.

Wittgenstein, L., Anscombe, G. E. M., & Wright, G. H. v. (1969). *On certainty.* Oxford: Blackwell.

Worth, J. (2014a) Unpublished interview. 4 December.

Worth, J. (2014b) *DML2014 – Featured Session 1 – Open Technologies for Learning* [video file]. Retrieved from: https://www.youtube.com/watch?v=6m90BzVVPG4.

Yonseienglish (2012). *Michael J. Sandel at Yonsei University in Seoul, South Korea* [video file]. 1 June. Retrieved from: https://www.youtube.com/watch?v=gMY08rgqYzc.

Yorke, M. (2010). Employability: aligning the message, the medium and academic values. *Journal of Teaching and Learning for Graduate Employability, 1*(1), 2–12.

Zhao, H. (2010). Investigating learners' use and understanding of peer and teacher feedback on writing: A comparative study in a Chinese English writing classroom. *Assessing Writing, 15*(1), 3–17.

Zhukov, K. (2012). Teaching strategies and gender in instrumental studios. *International Journal of Music Education, 30*(1), 32–45.

Zimmerman, B. J. (1989). A social cognitive view of self-regulated academic learning. *Journal of Educational Psychology, 81*(3), 329–39.

Zimmerman, B. J. (1998a). Developing self-fulfilling cycles of academic regulation: An analysis of exemplary instructional models. In D. Schunk & B. J. Zimmerman (Eds) *Self-regulated learning: from teaching to self-reflective practice* (pp.1–19). New York: Guildford Press.

Zimmerman, B. J. (1998b). Academic studying and the development of personal skill: A self-regulatory perspective. *Educational Psychologist, 33*(2–3), 73–86.

Zimmerman, B. J. (2000). Self-efficacy: An essential motive to learn. *Contemporary Educational Psychology, 25*(1), 82–91.

Zimmerman, B. J. (2002). Becoming a self-regulated learner: An overview. *Theory into Practice, 41*(2), 64–70.

Zimmerman, B. J. (2011). Motivational sources and outcomes of self-regulated learning and performance. In. B. J. Zimmerman & D. H. Schunk (Eds) *Handbook of self-regulation of learning and performance* (pp.49–64). New York: Routledge.

Zimmerman, B. J., & Bandura, A. (1994). Impact of self-regulatory influences on writing course attainment. *American Educational Research Journal, 31*(4), 845–62.

Zimmerman, B. J., Bandura, A., & Martinez-Pons, M. (1992). Self-motivation for academic achievement: The role of self-efficacy and personal goal setting. *American Educational Research Journal, 29*, 663–76.

Zimmerman, B. J., & Kitsantas, A. (2002). Acquiring writing revision and self-regulatory skill through observation and emulation. *Journal of Educational Psychology, 94*, 660–8.

Zimmerman, B. J., & Martinez-Pons, M. (1986). Development of a structured interview for assessing student use of self-regulated learning strategies. *American Educational Research Journal, 23*(4), 614–28.

Zimmerman, B. J., & Martinez-Pons, M. (1988). Construct validation of a strategy model of student self-regulated learning. *Journal of Educational Psychology, 80*, 284–90.

Zimmerman, B. J., & Martinez-Pons, M. (1990). Student differences in self-regulated learning: Relating grade, sex, and giftedness to self-efficacy and strategy use. *Journal of Educational Psychology, 82*(1), 51–9.

Index

Note: Page numbers in bold highlight sections of text that are key or provide a definition of that index topic